Dear Reader,

We hope you enjoy reading this book.

Should you have any questions, would like to know more about the Jewish perspective on the Afterlife or other topics in Jewish understanding or practice, please contact us at **thejewishafterlife@gmail.com**.

This book is provided in memory of
ELIEZER BEN YITZCHOK z"L
לעילוי נשמת ר' אליעזר בן ר' יצחק ז"ל

Afterlife

THE JEWISH VIEW

Where are we headed?

Afterlife

THE JEWISH VIEW
Where are we headed?

JONATHAN MORGENSTERN
With extended footnotes and a foreword by
Rabbi Sholom Kamenetsky

MOSAICA PRESS

Mosaica Press, Inc.

© 2014 by Mosaica Press

Edited by Doron Kornbluth

Typeset and designed by Rayzel Broyde

All rights reserved

ISBN 13: 978-1-937887-25-4   ISBN-10: 1937887251

Published and distributed by:

Mosaica Press, Inc.

www.mosaicapress.com

info@mosaicapress.com

Dedicated to the Memory of

Gail Natalie Morgenstern

(July 8, 1943 – September 6, 2004)

Arthur Bruce Morgenstern

(December 19, 1939 – May 24, 2000)

Table of Contents

Acknowledgements 9

Foreword 11

Introduction 15

Welcome to the Afterlife 21

What is the Purpose of Life? 24

What Happens When We Die? 27

Reincarnation 44

Who Am "I"? 48

A Deeper Look at the World's Four Stages of Existence 52

This World and the "Secret of Life" 53

The World of Souls: A Temporary Post-death Abode 63

Messiah: Step One in Bridging This World to the World to Come ... 71

Resurrection: Step Two in Bridging This World
to the World to Come 76

The World to Come - Our Eternal Existence 85

Why is the Afterlife Relevant? 93

Appendix: אבן שלמה

Acknowledgements

I prepared this work in memory of my parents, **Gail and Arthur Morgenstern**, who epitomized the importance of refining one's moral character and achieving the maximum with each day of life.

The information and explanations in this work are largely based on the teachings and lectures of **HaRav Sholom Kamenetsky**, Rosh Yeshivah of the Talmudical Yeshiva of Philadelphia, who based his teachings on his extensive study of these issues as addressed in the Talmud and other parts of our tradition.

Words cannot fully express the amount of spiritual light and strength he has provided to me and my family. I am deeply grateful for the relationship Hashem has granted me with him, and for his enthusiasm, encouragement, and efforts to bring this work to its fruition.

Thank you to **Jon Erlbaum** for spending a significant amount of time reviewing, editing, and providing a unique perspective on this work. I am blessed to have a friend and learning partner like you.

My deep appreciation goes to the entire staff of Mosaica Press. Under the guidance of **Rav Yaacov Haber,** Mosaica has done a superb job helping to visualize, create, prepare, improve, and refine this book. I cannot recommend them enough. In particular, **Rabbi Doron Kornbluth**, Mosaica's senior editor, has been a full partner in this project — it is hard to imagine the book coming to fruition without his energy, enthusiasm, and professional skill.

Thank you to my wife for helping simplify some of the ideas in this work, helping me grow as a person, and for being my partner in life!

And with deep appreciation I thank Hashem for all the blessings that He has bestowed upon me.

Jonathan Morgenstern
Philadelphia
5774 (2013)

Foreword

It is with trepidation, yet with a sense of urgency, that I pen this foreword. Trepidation, because of the nature of the subject matter in this small book. Urgency, because this book is long overdue.

I was privileged to have had the chance to meet a very special individual: Arthur B. Morgenstern. We established a time to learn Torah daily as he established his reconnection to his roots. One of the burning issues and questions he had was: What is the eschatological system that the Torah views? Is there a world beyond? Where does one go after death? These, and other questions of this sort, had us learning the classical Jewish sources that discussed these very interesting subjects.

There was, however, one catalyst that gave our discussions more urgency. One of Art's family members died and another family member decided to cremate the deceased. Art tried his best to persuade his relatives to provide the deceased a burial in accordance to Jewish law, but to no avail. The complete ignorance of Jewish belief in an "Afterlife" simply didn't allow for any discussion. It broke Art's spirit to see his family member cremated. In his compassion for others, and as a merit for the deceased, Art initiated a project: He felt that there was a desperate need to educate the general public on these issues.

As difficult as these subjects are to address, they are crucial to be disseminated — simply to allow for educated decisions.

Art and I started our project by recording a question-and-answer session between ourselves. Art would ask all the hard questions and I would try to answer, keeping in mind that I was addressing an audience with no Jewish education whatsoever. This formed the core of what we felt would eventually be a book geared to the secular public to help them understand and make informed decisions.

Unfortunately, God had other plans.

After a brief illness, Art's soul returned to its Creator. As time passed, our original dream to disseminate the Torah's view on the Afterlife and the importance of Jewish burial became a more distant dream.

But again, God had different plans.

Art's son, Jonathan, as part of his own personal search, picked up the gauntlet from where we left off. In his own course of life, Jon has come across many types of Jews, from all walks of life, that all share a common curiosity: What is the Jewish belief about the Afterlife? Where do we go after we die? Is there really a belief in resurrection? Do Jews believe in reincarnation? And the list goes on.

We are all naturally curious to know about the obscure and mystical world of souls and the Afterlife. Yet it is a subject seldom discussed and poorly understood. With God's help, I was privileged to learn these deep and esoteric subjects and lecture about them extensively. The lectures were delivered to a highly educated audience over the course of four years. As with many topics within the realm of Torah, the information is expansive and contains many different opinions. Jon has managed to distill those lectures, follow-up questions, and conversations with me to clarify the material into a presentable book that the average reader can understand.

Being that there are different opinions about some of the issues discussed, we have avoided details and presented the ideas according to the consensus of opinions. The sources included can be used for further research.

My fervent hope is that the ideas presented in this book be read and reread, and will allow people to be more educated about their lives in general — and their "after-lives" in particular.

I would also like to thank Jon for working on this project, for bringing it to fruition, and for allowing me to finally honor my pledge to Art to disseminate the importance of Jewish burial and what follows.

Let the merits of increased awareness of the Afterlife be a merit to his soul.

Sholom Kamenetsky
Philadelphia
5774 (2013)

Introduction:
Death — the Elephant in Our Subconscious

Young children imagine that they will live forever. Then, one day, the child makes an [indelible] discovery. Someone he knows...passes away, and the child is shocked into reality: life comes to an end.

Slowly, it dawns on the child that what happened to others will happen to him; someday, he too will die. And as his fantasy of immortality fades, a bit of childhood innocence vanishes forever.

Soon, the fearful shock gives way to questions....What is it like to die? What is death really like? The child grows and matures and learns to stifle his questions. They don't seem so urgent as he perceives how slowly time passes. They don't bother him so acutely, at least not now.

But [these questions] remain buried within him. Indeed, it remains deep within all of us. And we worry; what is it like to pass through the gates of death? What will we experience when our time comes?[1]

MY FATHER'S DEATH — REMOVING MY SENSE OF IMMORTALITY

In May 2000, my father passed away at the age of sixty. I was thirty-one at the time. He was diagnosed with an unknown primary

---

1   *Encounters*, Rabbi Aryeh Kaplan, p.18, Moznaim publishing Corp. 1990, with permission.

cancer just six weeks earlier. We were caught by surprise. He was in great shape, ate well, and exercised regularly. A vibrant person, it seemed like he might live until one hundred.

After his passing, I realized that while my father was still alive, his presence in my life created a subconscious barrier between me and death. Up until then I had cruised through life, not actively considering the fact that my years in this world were limited. I had not given any thought to spiritual matters. His brief illness and untimely passing impacted me sharply.

Suddenly, I felt like I was "next in line." My mortality became an immediate issue. I needed to know whether my consciousness — my soul — would exist after I died. And, if so, what is the "Afterlife" like?

CREMATION IN THE FAMILY — A CATALYST TO EDUCATE OTHERS

In 1999, my father, Arthur, and his rabbi, Rav Sholom Kamenetsky, began a project to educate Jews about the Jewish views on the Afterlife. The catalyst of this endeavor was the recognition that most Jews know very little, if anything, about these issues. Most of us do not understand how fundamental the idea of an Afterlife is to Jewish identity — and why this knowledge is extremely relevant to our lives.

Specifically, my father became aware that several of our relatives were considering cremation — something not particularly unreasonable if the person never really looked into the significance of the issues involved. If costs and logistics are the only considerations, cremation may sometimes seem like an easy way to "get rid of" the body.

What our relatives didn't realize was that there is much more at stake than simple practicalities. According to Jewish thought, the physical body is essential to the very concept of a human being,[2] and cremation is therefore prohibited.[3] The body is the vessel that houses the soul.[4] It is the fusion of body and soul that provides an individual

---

2   *Derech Hashem* 3:2, *Da'as Tevunos* (42-76)
3   *Kol Bo on Aveilus* (3:21), *Gesher HaChaim* 16:9
4   *Sefer HaChinuch* 374

free choice and his life in this world.[5] As a result, the body must be, and is accorded immense respect. Furthermore, we need our bodies even after our "earthly" deaths.[6]

As we will see, one of the details of the Afterlife is the literal rejoining of the deceased body with the disembodied soul (i.e., resurrection).[7] For this reason, an educated choice to be cremated is problematic.

Instead, the Torah (Bible) instructs us to "plant" the body in the ground.[8] In this way, burial acts as a necessary step in one's eventual "re-growth" and entry into the World to Come (our final and eternal state of existence).

Jews believe in *that?*

Most Jews are surprised to hear that in Jewish thought resurrection is seen as an integral component of the Afterlife.[9] At first the concept may seem bizarre, in the very least. We do not see human beings being resurrected.

That being said, perhaps the idea is deeper and more mature than horror movies — involving zombies coming back from the dead to attack us — depict. Is it really so hard to keep an open mind to the concept?

Imagine that an alien being came to visit Earth. His planet was totally different than ours and operated on completely different principles.

What would he think when someone would tell him about the concept of resurrection? Disbelief? Perhaps.

On the other hand, what would his reaction be when someone would tell him that he could plant a small pellet in the ground and in time a huge fruit-bearing tree would emerge? Probably the same level of disbelief.

---

5   *Nefesh HaChaim* 1:7
6   Ra'avid on *Yad, Teshuvah* 8:2, and so is found in most Rishonim and Kabbalists
7   *Sanhedrin* 91a
8   *Ibid.* 90b
9   Rambam, Commentary on *Sanhedrin* 10

In other words, to one not familiar with the way the Earth operates, what's the difference between planting a seed in the ground and expecting growth, and planting a body in the ground and expecting growth? Perhaps it just takes a lot longer for the implanted body to grow and, furthermore, no one has witnessed it yet.[10]

Ultimately, the act of planting — whether it is a seed or a body — is an act of faith.[11] The only difference is that, in the current state of our world, we physically witness seeds growing into trees.

BEING COMFORTED AT A FAMILY FUNERAL

I attended the funeral for my great-uncle a few years ago. It was a small graveside ceremony at which some of the family members spoke about the deceased, recalling his life and discussing his character traits. As he had lived into his nineties, the tone was not as sad as some other funerals I have attended. In a way, it was a beautiful moment as the family related memories and talked about the good qualities he embodied. But then the rabbi began to speak.

He spoke very kindly about the deceased. Yet, after every few sentences or so, he mentioned something about a possible Afterlife. Looking back, it seems to me now that his intention was to offer us comfort by emphasizing that life continues after death.

Unfortunately, despite being a rabbi, he wasn't knowledgeable — or himself convinced — about classic Jewish belief. The best he could do was to utter vague statements about his lack of knowledge, such as "but I don't know what happens next."

From my vantage point, the mood turned from somewhat uplifting to uneasy. It was a moment in which family and friends were seeking inspiration, continuity, and the silver lining. We all wanted to hear that our beloved was not gone but had just moved on to the next phase of his existence. It wouldn't have been appropriate to interject

---

10   *Michtav M'Eliyahu* Book 1
11   *Shabbos* 31a, Tosafos. s.v. Emunas

anything, but I so wanted to tell the mourners that Judaism most clearly *does* include belief in the Afterlife. The Torah itself hints to it, and our Oral Tradition discusses it extensively.

In fact, according to Jewish philosophy, death is merely the beginning of our ultimate reality. An existence of incomprehensible beauty and pleasure awaits the individual after death[12] — especially for someone who spent his years in this world wisely.[13]

This rabbi was not dissimilar to the majority of Jews today; he had never been taught the traditional Jewish belief regarding the Afterlife.

Jewish belief originates from God's revelation to the entire Jewish nation at Mount Sinai more than 3,300 years ago. It is predicated on the idea that humanity was created for the purpose of achieving spiritual growth in this world and earning eternal pleasure as a result.[14] We accomplish this by working to improve our character traits, learning Torah wisdom, and performing the *mitzvos* (commandments) to the best of our abilities.[15] Perhaps the most fundamental and empowering idea about the Afterlife is that each person creates his or her eternal world with every moment of existence in this world. In other words, we are fully in charge of our own destiny.[16]

The rest of this work is an expansion of this concept. It includes ideas and teachings regarding:

- How individual souls and the world at large arrive at the final state of the World to Come; and
- How our current world and the World to Come are intimately connected.

My parents recognized that our short time in this world is a gift,

---

12   *Avos* 4:17
13   *Ibid.* 4:16
14   *Mesilas Yesharim* 1
15   *Ibid.*
16   *Ruach Chaim* (R' Chaim Volozhin) on Introduction to *Avos*: "All of Israel has a share in the World to Come."

but only to the extent we appreciate it as such. By integrating the idea that there is something to live for — besides the here-and-now — we grow in our ability to appreciate the gift of life and we grow spiritually. I hope you find these teachings informative and uplifting.

Welcome to the Afterlife...

...Please check all previous knowledge about the Afterlife (that comes from movies, popular books, and television) at the front door.

Most of us realize — at least deep inside ourselves — that there is more to this world than what meets the eye. Even if we somehow knew for a fact that we would never be caught, we wouldn't commit murder; we sense that life is meaningful beyond what our eyes and ears tell us. Deep down, we know that there is something beyond.

Still, authentic information about spirituality and the Afterlife is not always easily available. As a result, we are left with doubts. Many of us lack the knowledge as to whether Judaism even postulates an Afterlife, much less the details, implications, or importance of that belief.

As a starting point, it should be noted that all monotheistic belief derives from Judaism. Judaism is the only belief system even claiming to be founded on God's revelation to an entire nation. It is the source of wisdom and knowledge about true spirituality. Yet, since we don't have adequate time and motivation to explore what Judaism says on these issues, we are left to glean ideas from what filters through the public media, which rarely (if ever) is aligned with Jewish thought. As a result, we are led astray. Given what the world at large disseminates about the Afterlife — and God in general — most Jews are understandably skeptical and therefore reject these ideas.

Television, movies, and books convey images such as a peaceful world of clouds enclosed by pearly gates, a fiery purgatory ruled by a pitchfork-wielding demon, and zombies coming out of graves. These ideas — even if appearing in works of fiction — severely distort authentic spiritual concepts about the Afterlife. Common sense tells us that these cannot be true as represented. Furthermore, the imagery is ridiculous, which makes the true concepts seem all the more like fiction. And what is the result of our exposure to this? We become desensitized to important Jewish beliefs and lose interest in pursuing an understanding of the Afterlife and finding how it relates to our current life.

Most Jews are surprised to learn that heaven, hell, Satan, and resurrection are all concepts that originate in Jewish belief. Of course, the original, accurate, and beautiful Jewish teachings on these subjects are fundamentally different than what one would conclude based on the portrayals offered by public media and other religions.

For example: in Jewish thought there is no devil with a pitchfork. Instead, "Satan" is associated with the negative inclination that resides within each human being. Its purpose within God's plan is to provide us with tests and temptations in an attempt to elevate us to higher levels of growth and reward.

One more: hell is not a fiery place in the bowels of the Earth or a vindictively punitive concept of eternal damnation. Instead, *Gehinnom* (as it is called in Hebrew) is a temporary place whose primary purpose is purification. It is analogous to a hospital. No one desires being in a hospital, but if part of one's body needs repair, thank God there is such a place that allows one to get better and go on living.

Similarly, if one didn't live his life in a way that allowed his soul to fully partake in the pleasure of the World to Come, thank God there is a place for purification. It is important to note that one can't and shouldn't act haphazardly in this world and rely on *Gehinnom* to fix one's mistakes — one can only be purified in accordance with the level that he has attained in this world.

The point is that beautiful and holy Jewish teachings on these matters do exist, but have been radically altered by modern media and imagery. Let us explore the original Jewish teachings.

What is the Purpose of Life?

In order to put the Jewish beliefs on the Afterlife into the proper context, we need to appreciate why we were created. Judaism does not postulate an afterworld that is unrelated to this one. On the contrary, each person's Afterlife is the direct outgrowth of his life in this world. Once we leave this world, we will exist forever in a new dimension as the person we have become.[17]

Let's ask two important questions:

1) Why did God create the world?

Being Infinite and lacking any imperfection whatsoever, God has no needs. Consequently, then, He could not possibly have created the world for Himself.

Judaism therefore teaches that God is the Ultimate Giver and created the world and humanity in order to share His Goodness with others.[18] He created the world for us. If so...

2) Why didn't God just *give* us His goodness in a beautiful, easy, spiritually perfect world? Why put us into this world that has so much pain and challenges?

Being Infinite and lacking any limitations whatsoever, He

---

17   *Ruach Chaim* (R' Chaim Volozhin) on Introduction to *Avos*: "All of Israel has a share in the World to Come."

18   Kuf Lamed Ches *Pischei Chochma* 2:2

undoubtedly could have provided the ability for people to receive His Goodness without having to go through the difficulty of this world.

So why didn't He?

God knew that in order for one to truly appreciate something, one must feel the accomplishment of earning it. As is often said, the harder you work for something, the more you appreciate it. In order to maximize our spiritual connection and to make it real, we need to "own" our spirituality rather than just receive it as a handout. By working hard to improve and grow, our spiritual growth becomes intrinsic to who we are, and therefore we become more real, lasting, and God-like. His greatest gift was giving us the opportunity for growth. God made this concept His basis for creating the world.[19]

This idea that we need to "earn" the ultimate good helps explain the connection between the current world and the afterworld. This world is the only time to earn reward, while the afterworld is the primary time for receiving reward.[20] The more effort we invest in being a good person and following God's guidance for a successful life in this world (i.e., Torah and *mitzvos*), the more we are rewarded in this life and the afterworld.[21]

THIS WORLD IS DIFFICULT — YET PERFECT TO ACCOMPLISH GOD'S PLAN

Why do bad things happen to good people? Why do bad things happen to anyone at all? We see innocent children suffering and it just doesn't seem right. With illness, poverty, and hatred, there's so much pain. If God exists, how can He allow this?

These are very deep and complex questions. At a very high level, the reason why people experience difficulty and pain in this world is closely related to the purpose of Creation. If the purpose of this world is to develop a connection with the Infinite and earn reward,

---

19   *Da'as Tevunos* (1-42)
20   *Avodah Zarah* 3a
21   *Avos* 5:22

then we must have a mechanism to earn that reward, i.e., through making a choice.

This choice is whether to recognize God's existence and follow His guidance for us, or not to do so. In order to be a real choice, the options must be equally balanced, even if that means this world is not easy and comfortable.

If we were to live in a world where people could fall off buildings and not get hurt, would we really have a true choice? What if we were to see the cosmic benefits of listening to His instructions, e.g., — if every time someone did a *mitzvah* (commandment/good deed), he was rewarded on the spot? It would be too obvious that a Higher Power was in control. There would be no real choice. We would essentially be robots, not really *earning* much at all, and the entire purpose of Creation would be nullified.

Providing human beings an environment that allows free moral choice is another of God's guiding principles for this world. This is why God's presence is not manifested in the world and the world seemingly operates according to a natural order — with all the tornadoes, hurricanes, illnesses, and other difficulties that we know all too well. This world has many challenges, some of them exceedingly difficult and painful, all because it is only a preparation for the goal of Creation, which is the World to Come.[22]

What Happens When We Die?

Human history is a progression to an eternal world that will be reached in the World to Come...each individual progresses to his eternal reward via a series of stages that follow earthly death.[23]

According to Jewish thought, a human being is comprised of two components: a physical body and a spiritual soul.[24] The body and soul are opposites in nature, but are fused together to provide us life and consciousness as we know it.[25]

The body desires physical pleasures and gravitates towards laziness and inaction. The soul desires meaning, growth, transcendence, and a connection with the Infinite.[26] These two conflicting components operate in partnership within each person.

When a person dies, the body and soul are separated.[27] The soul (and consciousness of the person) enters a new dimension of existence appropriately called the World of Souls (*Olam HaNeshamos*).[28] The World of Souls is a temporary existence in which souls are purified

---

23 Appendix to Artscroll's *Talmud Bavli Sanhedrin* (vol. III)
24 *Sanhedrin* 91a-b
25 Rema on *Orach Chaim* 6:1
26 *Koheles* 3:21
27 *Sanhedrin* 91
28 *Toras HaAdam*, Sha'ar HaGemul (Ramban)

as needed and then experience bliss in preparation for their eternal existence.[29]

While this is happening in the World of Souls, our present world continues onward. At a certain point in time in the future (and through a series of events), our present world will also undergo a fundamental change: it will become spiritually elevated.[30] Our Physical World will merge with the Spiritual World of Souls.[31] This will happen during a period of time called the Era of Resurrection.[32] During this period, human beings will, literally, be reconstituted. Their souls will be taken from the World of Souls and rejoined with their original (albeit purified) bodies.[33] It is after this resurrection process that the world and humanity will enter the final state of existence: The World to Come.[34]

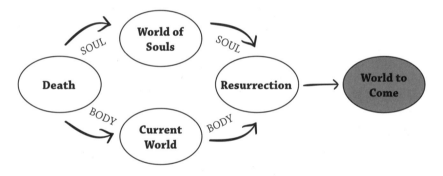

To summarize very simply:
1. A person dies;
2. his soul enters the World of Souls;
3. at resurrection he reenters our current world, which has been spiritually elevated; and
4. we exist eternally in the World to Come.

---

29   *Ibid.*
30   *Leshem Shebo VeAchloma, Sefer HaDeah* 2:4:12:9
31   *Ibid.*
32   *Ibid.*
33   *Ibid.*
34   *Ibid.*

This system is, of course, much deeper and more sophisticated than the basic description above. Let us focus more on three key concepts pertaining to the Afterlife:

1. The World of Souls
2. The world's four stages of existence
3. Reward and punishment

1. The World of Souls

Death is defined as the **temporary** separation of body and soul. For a period of time after death, the body goes to one place and the soul to another.

THE BODY

After death, an individual's body is buried in the ground. The purpose of burial is akin to the concept of planting.[35] Consider what happens when we plant a tiny seed. It first decomposes, and then undergoes a growth process to become something quite different and much greater than its original form. Similarly, at death, the human body is implanted into the earth for the purpose of an eventual regrowth into a new body — a spiritual body that is quite different than the body we currently know. This new body will have the ability to rejoin with the soul and experience an eternal existence.

THE SOUL

After death, the soul enters a dimension of spiritual existence called the World of Souls. The World of Souls is the residence for these after-death souls which are now body-less. It is a place of purification (if needed), spiritual growth, and partial reward. (Note that full reward occurs in the World to Come.)[36]

Souls that require purification first enter a part of the World of

---

35   *Sanhedrin* 90b
36   *Toras HaAdam*, Sha'ar haGemul (Ramban)

Souls called *Gehinnom*. Depending on the need for purification, most souls remain there from one second to one year, after which they reside in another part of the World of Souls called *Gan Eden* (the Garden of Eden).[37]

In *Gan Eden*, the soul experiences sublime pleasures to the extent it has merited them with the person's actions in this world. The disembodied soul remains in *Gan Eden* until the world we know progresses to the Era of Resurrection of the Dead (discussed below), at which point bodies and souls are rejoined.

TRANSITIONING FROM THIS WORLD TO THE NEXT

At death, a person transitions from a world infused with both physical and spiritual elements to a fully Spiritual World. What a person experiences during this transition depends on which aspects of life one identified with — body or soul.

Was the person a slave to his bodily desires? Was his soul largely in control, or was he somewhere in between?

For one who lived as a more "spiritual" person in this world, the transition may be quite easy.

For one who lived a more "animalistic" life, the transition may be more difficult.[38] Each person will confront the realization of his true purpose in life in contrast to what he actually invested his being and energies in.[39]

The Talmud discusses the two aspects of the World of Souls that were mentioned above: *Gan Eden* and *Gehinnom*. It notes that *Gan Eden* is a pleasure-based experience, while *Gehinnom* is quite the opposite — a difficult place created for purification.[40] Interestingly, the *Baalei Mussar* (those who are involved with the ethical teachings of Judaism) relate that the difference between the two is but a hairsbreadth.

---

37   *Eduyos* 2:10
38   *Berachos* 8a
39   See *Even Sheleyma* (Gr"a) 10:11
40   *Leshem ad loc.*

How can two things that seem to be polar opposites actually be almost the same?

A man nearing death had a dream that an angel appeared to him and offered to grant him a wish. The man asked the angel to show him what things are like after death. The angel agreed to provide him a preview.

The angel led the man down a long corridor, at the end of which were two magnificent doors. The doors opened into a great banquet hall. As far as the man could see were beautifully decorated tables laden with the finest meats, breads, fruits, drinks, and delicacies. The man was very comforted with this vision of what he thought was heaven.

But as he walked farther, he realized that all the residents in the room were not happy. And despite the banquet, they appeared hungry. The angel explained that this was not heaven. "You see, in the Afterlife, people do not have elbows. They cannot feed themselves. Furthermore, the people here did not learn to become givers in their lifetime. As a result, they cannot feed others here either."

The angel then took the man to visit heaven, where the man witnessed the same exact setting — a beautiful banquet with luscious delicacies. But in this banquet, everyone looked joyous. Some were dancing and singing, and everyone was talking and laughing as they fed each other with their outstretched (elbow-less) arms.

This is the essence of the World of Souls. One who has become sensitive to spirituality will enjoy unbelievable bliss. But one who let himself be a slave to physicality and developed no connection to spirituality will be incapable of experiencing pleasure in a purely spiritual environment. His consciousness will be seeking the physical stimuli he became accustomed to in this world. Yet it will not have the ability to quench those desires because they don't exist in that Spiritual World.

To be clear, physicality is not inherently bad. We were put into a physical world in order to use physicality for positive purposes. Note that Judaism has no convents and frowns on abstinence and unnecessary fasting in almost all cases. Eating a delicious meal on Shabbat is a mitzvah. The goal is not to deny the physical world. We can and should enjoy it and use it well. Physicality is only problematic when it becomes an end in itself.

The point is that at death, all of a person's physical achievements (e.g., fame, wealth) are left behind. On the other hand, his spiritual achievements (e.g., impact on others, personal growth, Torah, charity and other *mitzvos*) are permanent and represent the "currency" for experiencing bliss in the World to Come.

LIFE IN THE WORLD OF SOULS

Because we live in a limited, physical world, it is not possible to accurately describe what the next world is like. However, Rabbi Aryeh Kaplan, a twentieth century master of Judaism's esoteric traditions, attempts to give us some allusions to what this experience may be like. In his article "Naked Before God" he writes:[41]

What is it like to be a disembodied soul? How does it feel to be in the World of Souls?

We know that the human brain, marvelous organ that it is, is still very inefficient as a thinking device. Henri Bergson has suggested that one of the main functions of the brain and nervous system is to eliminate activity and awareness, rather than produce it.

Aldous Huxley quotes Prof C.D. Broad's comments on this. He says that every person is capable of remembering everything that has ever happened to him. He is able to perceive everything that surrounds him. However, if all this information poured into our minds at once, it would overwhelm us. So the function of the brain and nervous system is to protect us and prevent us from being overwhelmed and confused by the vast amount of information that impinges upon our sense organs. They shut out most of what we perceive and remember. All that would confound us is eliminated and only the small, special selection that is useful is allowed to remain.

Huxley explains that our mind has powers of perception and concentration that we cannot even begin to imagine. But our main business is to

---

41   *If You Were God*, Aryeh Kaplan, p. 29–32, OU/NCSY Publications, 1983, with permission.

survive at all costs. To make survival possible, all of our mind's capabilities must be funneled through the reducing valve of the brain.

Some researchers are studying this effect. They believe that this reducing-valve effect may be very similar to the jamming equipment used to block out offensive radio broadcasts. The brain constantly produces a kind of static, cutting down our perception and reducing our mental activity.

This static can actually be seen. When you close your eyes, you see all sorts of random pictures flashing through your mind. It is impossible to concentrate on any one of them for more than an instant, and each image is obscured by a host of others superimposed over it.

This static can even be seen when your eyes are opened. However, one usually ignores these images since they are so faint compared to our visual perception. However, they still reduce one's perception, both of the world around him and of himself.

Much of what we know about this static is a result of research done with drugs that eliminate it. According to a number of authorities, this is precisely how the psychedelic drugs work.

Now imagine the mental activity of a disembodied soul, standing naked before God. The reducing valve is gone entirely. The mind is open and transparent. Things can be perceived in a way that is impossible to a mind held back by a body and nervous system. The visions and understanding are the most delightful bliss imaginable...

But then, an individual will also see himself in a new light. Every thought and memory will be lucid, and he will see himself for the first time without the static and jamming that shuts out most thoughts.

Even in our mortal physical state, looking at oneself can sometimes be pleasing and at other times very painful. Certain acts leave us proud and pleased with ourselves. Others cause excruciating pains, especially when we are caught.

Imagine standing naked before God, with your memory wide open, completely transparent without any jamming mechanism or reducing valve to diminish its force. You will remember everything you ever did and see it in a new light. You will see it in the light of the unshaded spirit or, if you will, in God's own light that shines from one end of Creation to the other. The memory of every good deed will be the sublimest of pleasures, as our tradition speaks of the World to Come.

But your memory will also be open to all the things of which you are ashamed. They cannot be rationalized away or dismissed. You will be facing yourself, fully aware of the consequences of all your deeds. We all know the terrible shame and humiliation experienced when one is caught in the act of doing something wrong. Imagine being caught by one's own memory with no place to escape... A number of our great teachers write that the fire of netherworld is actually the burning shame one experiences because of his sins.

We are taught that the judgment of the wicked lasts twelve months. Even the naked soul can gradually learn to live with this shame and forget it, and the pain eventually subsides. It may be more than coincidence that twelve months is also the length of time required for something to be forgotten in Talmudic law. Thus one mourns a parent for twelve months, and says a special blessing upon seeing a close friend after this period of time. Of course, there is an exception to this rule. There are the nonbelievers and worst of sinners reckoned in the Talmud. These individuals have nothing else but their shame and have no escape from everlasting torment.

2. The world's four stages of existence

To put the entirety of Creation into context, the Talmud teaches of four distinct stages of existence. In essence, these are time periods for the world:

1. The current world
2. The Messianic Era
3. The Era of Resurrection
4. The World to Come

Jewish tradition teaches that our current world is temporary and the next two stages (the Messianic Era and the Era of Resurrection) are essentially transitional phases. The World to Come is an eternal state of existence, and the goal of all Creation. Still, it is not a separate place from our current world.

Rather, the World to Come parallels our world, and in fact inhabits our world, but on a spiritually dominant plane of existence that is not limited by the bounds of space and time in the way that we currently experience them. In other words, it exists here right now. It's just that we are unable to fully access it yet.

Our current world does not need to disappear in order to enter that dimension of existence. It simply needs to be elevated. This occurs via the stages of existence which precede it and as a result of our choices and actions.

1. This World

We live our lives in this world. It is the only world that we can readily sense and understand. This world is full of pleasure, pain, and challenges. It is the perfect setting for us to be tested, earn reward, and fulfill God's ultimate plan.[42] In the section below ("This world and The Secret of Life") we will discuss the spiritual realties which are embedded into our world.

2. The Messianic Era

Our current world needs to go through a growth/purification process to be prepared for the eternal existence of the World to Come, just as individual bodies and souls do. This occurs via two transition "stages": the Messianic Era and the Era of Resurrection of the Dead.[43]

The first transition stage is called the Messianic Era. In this epoch, a Jewish man (a descendant of King David) will unify the Jewish People, become their king, and rebuild the Holy Temple in Jerusalem.[44] As a direct result of these achievements, the knowledge of God will fill the world to such an extent that the entire world will realize its beauty and live according to God's will as communicated in

---

42   *Da'as Tevunos* 72
43   *Leshem ad loc.*
44   *Yad, Melachim* 11:1

His Torah.[45] The result of doing so will be the peaceful coexistence of all people on Earth.[46] As a direct result of living by the Torah, the entire creation will begin a transformation process into a spiritually dominant world that is capable of lasting eternally.[47]

During the Messianic Era — a forty-year period — the world will still exist as we know it. There will not be a change in the natural world order; the sun, moon, and rest of nature will function as they do today.[48] The only change that will occur is that the Jewish nation will no longer be subjugated to the nations of the world.[49] Anti-Semitism and religious hatred will disappear. The Jewish People will be physically, emotionally, and spiritually free to serve God without obstruction.[50]

Belief in the Messianic Era is one of the thirteen fundamental principles of Jewish belief outlined by Maimonides.[51] Why is it such a critical element of Jewish belief?

The explanation is quite profound. Because this era is a catalyst towards a new and better world, it teaches that our current state of existence is suboptimal. Without world peace, without humanity working together to make our world a better place, and without the ubiquitous appreciation of God's role in the world, we are far from the ideal way of life. Belief in the Messianic future is an elusive concept in our fast-paced world. Many fail to realize that we are currently living in exile.

3. The Era of Resurrection of the Dead

The second transition stage is the Era of Resurrection of the Dead, in which the world continues its transformation into a spiritually dominant existence.

At the beginning of this era, people will still live and die as we know today. Concurrently, a resurrection process begins. Souls which have

---

45   *Yeshayahu* 11:9
46   *Yeshayahu* 11:6; see *Yad ad loc.*
47   *Leshem ad loc.*
48   *Pesikta Rabasi* 1
49   *Berachos* 34b
50   *Ibid.*
51   Rambam, commentary on *Sanhedrin* 10

undergone a purification process through burial and regrowth and have resided in the World of Souls will now be reunited with their bodies.

As a result, the world's population will become mixed with both "normal" and resurrected people. Eventually, all the remaining "normal" people will die and only the resurrected will exist.

Unlike the Messianic Era, this Era of Resurrection is a time of supernatural existence where the world experiences miracles that depart from the natural order and fundamentally alter and elevate the world.[52]

The idea of resurrection is **not** that the dead will be brought back to life to resume the lives they had previously lived. Rather, the concept is that everyone who ever died will be brought back to live the way they should have. They will thus extract the maximum spiritual benefit from their lives according to the spiritual truths God implanted into our existence. As a direct consequence of living by the Torah and its *mitzvos*, humanity will activate the purification necessary to transform our earthly world into a spiritual dimension capable of entering the eternal paradise of the World to Come.[53]

This is another one of Maimonides's thirteen fundamental principles of Jewish belief. Why is it so critical? The concept of resurrection teaches that every single moment of existence is valuable, and that nothing — not a single moment — gets lost. Furthermore, it reinforces the idea that our bodies and physicality are important. As previously noted, it was God's plan to create us in a physical world with physical bodies. By putting us in a physical world, God wanted us to choose to actualize our spiritual potential from within a challenging setting. And as the result of doing so, we become a partner in completing His Creation.[54]

4. The World to Come

After the Messianic and Resurrection Eras, the world will have

---

52 *Leshem ad loc.*
53 *Ibid.*
54 *Derech Hashem, Da'as Tevunos*

been transformed into one that can exist eternally. At this point, a Final Judgment will take place to measure the cumulative impact of one's actions. This Final Judgment will usher in the World to Come — our eternal existence where each individual experiences the transcendent pleasures he has merited via his actions in this world. The eternity of the World to Come is not an infinitely long succession of moments (similar to how we experience this world), but a qualitatively unique existence beyond our concepts of time and space.[55]

Interestingly, there is a Divine time frame for all these era to occur. Just like a week has six days before the Sabbath, so too will the world exist for 6,000 years before its Sabbath, i.e. the World to Come. For this reason, all the events preceding the World to Come (Messiah, Resurrection, and Final Judgment) take place prior to the year 6,000 according to the Jewish calendar. At the time of this writing, we are in the year 5774.

3. Reward and Punishment

Reward and punishment is a fundamental principle of Jewish belief. Jewish tradition teaches that God

- Knows our thoughts and actions,
- Made His will known to us (via the revelation of Torah), and
- Provided us free will to choose between good and evil.

Therefore, it is logical that He rewards each individual with precision according to his deeds. Why should a person who chooses evil get the same eternal reward as a person who chooses good? Why should a person who is lazy and does little to connect to spirituality, improve himself, or change the world get the same reward as someone who puts in a lifetime of effort? Belief in a just God necessitates belief in reward and punishment.

---

55   *Ruach Chaim*, Commentary on *Avos* 4:22

EXPERIENCING THE TOTAL IMPACT OF ONE'S ACTIONS

In this world, we live with a linear concept of time. Each passing moment becomes part of our past. While we can access various memories, we don't feel much pain or pleasure from most of them. They are just history.

Once we leave this world, we will no longer exist with the same concept of time. At that point, all of our life's thoughts, words, and actions will be in front of us simultaneously. Everything will be in the present. There will be no past or future.[56]

Furthermore, we will not only *be aware* of all that we've personally done. Rather, we will *exist with the knowledge* of all that resulted from our deeds. We will experience the **total impact of our actions**.

For instance, one day a young boy comes home from school after getting in trouble several times for misbehaving. His father had a very difficult day at work and was not in a good mood. When he hears about his son's misdeeds, the father has the urge to hit the child, or at least yell and scream at him. Instead, he overcomes his anger and doesn't lash out.

What are the results of the father's self-restraint? In this world, we cannot see the full impact of our actions. It is unlikely that the father will ever appreciate the magnitude of his self-restraint. Yet sometimes one small action can have major repercussions. Perhaps the boy expected to be severely reprimanded, but when the father restrained himself, he effectuated a major, positive impact on the child's development. Perhaps this event became ingrained in the son's psyche and resulted in him being a more patient and compassionate person for the rest of his life, passing on these traits to his children and grandchildren.

Aside from this, the reward in the Next World is that the father will experience the eternal, spiritual bliss associated with his act as well as all of the resultant impact of that action throughout the generations, and the more difficult the act, the greater the spiritual accomplishment.

---

56   *Emunos V'Deyos* 4:4

PURIFICATION IS TEMPORARY

Most individuals merit a share in the World to Come. Few people die without many merits.[57] However, those who have harmed their souls in this world through bad choices need to undergo purification after death in order to be prepared for the World to Come.

This purification is called *Gehinnom*. *Gehinnom* helps a person become more spiritual to the extent that he did not achieve this on his own in this world. *Gehinnom* is not punitive. The difficulties associated with purification are necessary to cleanse a person so that he may experience maximum pleasure thereafter. It is actually another form of kindness from God.[58]

This is not to say that a person can therefore ignore his spiritual obligations in this world, spend a limited amount of time in a painful dimension, and then receive maximum reward. The purification only allows each person to fully receive what he has earned.[59]

It is important to note that this period of purification is temporary, unlike the non-Jewish concept of eternal damnation in hell. Once a soul reaches the eternal stage of the World to Come, it will experience only pleasure.[60]

INFINITE DEGREES OF REWARD/PURIFICATION

In the Afterlife, both the World of Souls and the World to Come, the intensity of bliss will vary according to the individual — depending on what he has merited in this world. The sages of the Torah indicate this with the dictum, "according to the effort is the reward."[61]

As this statement alludes to, one's reward is not just based on accomplishments. Results are in God's hands. Our reward is primarily determined by our actual efforts. Did we do our best to help the less fortunate? How much did we truly strive to become more spiritual people?

---

57   *Sanhedrin* 90a
58   *Nefesh HaChaim* 1:7
59   *Mesilas Yesharim* 4
60   See *Rosh HaShanah* 17a
61   *Avos* 5:22

CLEANING UP ONE'S SPIRITUAL RECORD

Although a person with misdeeds may need to undergo a purification process after death, this is only so for someone who did not purify himself in this world. It is much better and easier to undergo the process of change and forgiveness in this world. In Judaism, this concept is called *teshuvah* (literally, "return," as in "return to God"). The thrust of the idea is regretting one's misdeeds, verbalizing that regret to God, and resolving not to do those deeds again.[62]

Via proper *teshuvah*, one literally expends the spiritual effort to become a new person and thus justifiably deserves to have the misdeeds erased. The person is not the same person anymore and therefore doesn't need further purification.

Because he has changed on his own, this "new person" no longer requires undergoing difficulties after death.

Incredibly, if one does this out of love for God and the recognition of truth — as opposed to doing *teshuvah* out of fear of punishment — the prior sins are actually transformed into good deeds! How does this work? At a simple level, it is possible because those very misdeeds now serve as the inspiration for doing future good.[63]

It is far from easy to change one's essence or quit certain forms of negative behavior. This is why *teshuvah* is generally seen as a process.[63] This also explains why it circumvents the need for one to undergo purification after death. The hard work involved in changing oneself is **the equivalent in spiritual currency** to the suffering one would need to undergo in the next world (albeit in concentrated measure) if those negative behaviors remained unchanged.[64]

On a deeper level, those who do make positive changes in the here-and-now are not only averting future difficulties. They are doing exactly what is needed to build their individual portions in the World to Come. By growing spiritually, they will reap the benefits eternally.

---

62 *Sha'arei Teshuvah* 1
63 *Ibid.*
64 *Yoma* 86b

Interestingly, an additional benefit of trying to improve oneself and grow spiritually is that one is likely to experience more joy and meaning in this world as well. Being more aligned with one's individual life purpose in the world is the secret to feeling truly fulfilled and connected. Doing the right thing feels good. It allows us to continuously take pleasure from the incremental achievements towards becoming who we are supposed to be.[65]

FINAL THOUGHTS

Judaism teaches of an afterworld that (after death) we will clearly perceive as the ultimate goal of all of life. It will be more real than anything we currently know or experience. Since God's presence will be so immediately clear and manifest, we will no longer possess true free will and thus no longer be able to earn reward. We will, for eternity, enjoy the spiritual accomplishments and growth achieved during our lives.

How does knowing about the Afterlife impact me right now? How is it relevant? Why is it not just another nice piece of intellectual knowledge we can file away?

With each moment of life, we are "writing" our life story that will nourish us eternally. We can choose how the story will read. We can try to improve ourselves by overcoming and channeling our negative traits. We can use our speech more positively, uplift others (not ourselves), be less selfish, and bring more kindness to the world. We can strive to understand our Creator and His instructions for us, as He has communicated in the Torah.

A rich man's business went in the tank and he was barely able to feed his family. Fortunately, he found a benefactor to loan him the funds to restart his business. After one year the benefactor came to collect and found that the man had not touched the loan — it was just sitting in his closet. The benefactor felt insulted.

---

65   *Yalkut Shimoni, Devarim* 846

Likewise, the Almighty gives each of us a soul. He doesn't want us to return it to Him at the end of our days in the same condition that we received it, or worse. He wants us to undertake spiritual growth and enhance our souls. And ultimately, the loan must be repaid. What is truly ours in the World to Come is only the "profit" we've effectuated with our actions.

Reincarnation

Reincarnation is the belief that the soul, upon death, comes back to earth in another body or a different form. Like most other beliefs regarding the Afterlife, reincarnation has its roots in Jewish thought. And, not surprisingly, the Jewish understanding and details vary widely from mainstream Western perspectives.[66]

When we hear the term *reincarnation*, we naturally think that upon death, the person's soul — in its entirety — comes back to earth for another life, albeit in a different body. This is a misconception. A person, meaning an individual's consciousness, is unique. He has but one chance at life. That is why Judaism considers life so precious.

According to Jewish teachings, reincarnation is indeed about the spirit returning to this world in another physical form; however, it is not the returning of one's *entire* soul to another body or another form. Instead, what gets reincarnated is only a part of a person's soul — the part that has not completed its mission. Therefore, it is not accurate to say that a person gets reincarnated or that a person's soul gets reincarnated.[67]

The part of a person's soul that has achieved its mission moves

---

66   *Reishis Chochmah*, Sha'ar HaYirah 13 at length; see *Kehilas Ya'akov* in responsa to the author of *Malei Ro'im* on the subject of reincarnation, and also in responsa on the commentary of the Abarbanel (on the Torah) towards the end of *parshas Ki Seitzei* on the essence of *yibum*.

67   *Kehilas Ya'akov ad loc.*; Commentary of Gr"a on *Yonah*; Arizal, Sha'ar HaGilgulim. See also *Gilgulei Neshamos* (Ram"a MiPano)

on to its next residence in the World of Souls and what follows. This completed portion of soul remains as that person's unique identity for eternity. The portion of that person's soul that did not complete its mission is what becomes subject to reincarnation. This incomplete portion of soul is placed inside another body and becomes an entirely new person with a new consciousness. This new person is not the same as the first person. The first person has lost his opportunity to perfect the part of his soul that was formerly part of him. The knowledge of this lost opportunity is part of the remorse one experiences in the Next World.[68]

Although the reincarnated portion of one's soul is no longer part of that person and his unique identity, there will be a closer affinity between the two portions and they will recognize each other in the Next World. This is similar to how we have an affinity with our family members but exist as separate people.

WHY DO WE NEED REINCARNATION?

Reincarnation is necessary in order to complete the purpose of Creation. As we have seen, God created the world to share His goodness. As a result, He created Adam and Eve. If they would have heeded God's commandment, their combined soul would have remained pure and they would have entered the World to Come and merited eternal life in the form they were created.

Upon sinning, Adam and Eve damaged their souls.[69] As a result, they could not fully connect with God. Man's task after the sin became to repair the soul and elevate it to a state where it can truly be close to God.

Since man lives in a world with free will, and the option to choose to perform actions that damage (or at least do not repair) the soul exist, it is inevitable that humans will not always make optimal choices. The result is that many people are unlikely to *fully* repair the portion

---

68   See Gr"a *ad loc.*
69   *Sanhedrin* 38, and many places in *Derech Hashem*

of soul they were provided. Consequently, there needs to be a mechanism to allow mankind to continue the task of fixing the original soul in its entirety.[70]

WHY DO WE NEED BOTH REINCARNATION AND GEHINNOM?

How can we reconcile the existence of both reincarnation and *Gehinnom* (purification)? From what we've learned so far, both are mechanisms to repair the soul. As we've seen, the portion of the soul that completed its mission does not need reincarnation and will not experience it. If so, what purification in the World of Souls (*Gehinnom*) is still needed for it?

The explanation is that a soul may still require *Gehinnom* when it, in combination with the body, has performed positive actions that are capable of rectifying the soul, but the actions are tainted in some way.

For example, let's take an example of where someone performs the positive action of giving *tzedakah* (charity). He hands over the needed money, but instead of smiling and wishing the recipient well, he does something to make the taker ashamed about receiving the money. Granted, the giver has just performed a kindness and fulfilled the *mitzvah* of giving charity, and while he has done something very positive and tangible — thereby bringing his good intentions into the world — the action nonetheless exists with imperfections. He has incidentally caused an element of pain to the recipient. It must be cleansed in order to exist in the most pristine form.

This may be likened to someone who puts forth the effort to build a house but uses shoddy materials. The house has been built and can serve its purpose, but only to a limited extent. At some point in time it will need to undergo repairs to remain a viable structure.

This helps explain why even the successful or positive part of the soul still needs purification to perfect its good actions.

---

70   See Gr"a on *Mishlei* 11:4, 21:16; *Kehilas Ya'akov ad loc.*

Reincarnation, on the other hand, applies to the portion of soul that simply lacks performance of positive actions. In this case, there is no house to repair. Someone else must take the raw materials and build it. In other words, no rectification has taken place for that part of the soul. It must therefore enter another body to be purified and completed.[71]

---

71   Gr"a on *Mishlei* 6:31, 14:25, 22:7

Who Am "I"?

There is no more fundamental question than "Who am I?" We all use the words *I* and *me* to refer to ourselves. We live with a consciousness of self we refer to as *I*, but what exactly is it? This question may not be so simple, as each of us has thoughts, feelings, desires, a body, a spiritual side, and other components and sub-components.

Consider the famous philosophical dilemma: a doctor removes a person's brain and heart from his body, but keeps him "alive" via sophisticated technology and machines.

Let's say that the body is in one room of the hospital, the heart in another and the brain in yet a third room.

If asked, where would you say "the person" is?

This dilemma can be applied to each of us. Where exactly is the *I*? Furthermore, in the context of our discussion on death, the World of Souls, reincarnation, and resurrection, does the *I* change?

Rabbi Aryeh Kaplan addresses these questions in his article "Meet the Real You." He writes:[72]

Look at your hand. What do you see?

A part of your body, an appendage made of bone and sinew covered with flesh and skin. It is filled with nerves, blood vessels, and lymph ducts which run through it and connect it to your body, making it part of you.

You can open and close your hand. It obeys every command your mind

---

72   *If You Were God*, Aryeh Kaplan, *p.* 25–28, OU/NCSY Publications, 1983, with permission.

sends to it. It is yours — a part of you. But what are you? Who is the real you? What happens when you tell your hand to open and close? How does your mind will it to obey its commands?

Now point a finger at yourself. If you are an average person, you will point a finger at your chest. You think of yourself as your body. But is your body the real you?

Not too long ago, a person could consider his own body an integral part of himself. You were your body and your body was you. But this is no longer the case. Scientific progress has changed the entire concept of human personality and identity.

Heart transplants are now an almost commonplace occurrence. They do not even make the news any more. A man can live with another person's heart beating in his breast. If we would ask such a man to point to himself, would he point at his heart? Is this transplanted heart really part of him? Is the heart that beats within your breast the real you? Or is it something else entirely?

Researchers are predicting that within the next decade or two, brain transplants may be possible. This would force us to completely reevaluate the concept of human personality.

Imagine what it would be like to undergo a brain transplant. A man might be suffering from an incurable disease in his body, but still have a healthy brain. The donor, on the other hand, would have suffered irreparable brain damage, but otherwise have a perfectly sound body. The brain is removed from the sick body and placed in the healthy one.

Who is the new man? We have an old brain with all its memories, personality traits and behavior patterns. But it has a brand new body. The old body might have been old and sick, while the new one may be young and full of energy.

Let us ask this man to point to himself. Will he point to his body? Is the real you your body or your brain? ... A brain transplant raises enough questions. How about a memory transfer?

The science of cybernetics has discovered many similarities between computers and the human brain. Computer technology allows one to *program a memory transfer, taking all the information contained in one computer and transferring it to another. All that passes from one computer to the other is information.*

What if this were done to the human brain? This may lie in the realm of science fiction, but even if it will never be possible in practice, it is certainly possible in theory.

Let us try to envision such a memory transfer. Assume we have a person with an incurable disease where neither the body nor the brain can be salvaged. We clone a new body for this individual, brain and all. The possibilities of doing this have already been discussed at length in the literature. This new body has a blank, new brain, capable of functioning, but without any memories or thought patterns. As a final step, we accomplish a memory transfer, bringing all the information from the sick person into the brain of the new body.

We now have a fascinating situation. If all of a man's memories, thought patterns, and personality traits are transferred to a new body and brain, this person literally exists in his new body. But nothing physical has been transferred. No physical part of him has been placed in the new body. All that has been placed in this new body is information that previously existed in the old brain. Yet this information contains the sum total of this person's personality.

But if this is true, then it offers us tremendous new insight into our original question: Who is the real you?

The real you is not your body or brain, but the information contained in your brain — your memories, personality traits, and thought patterns.

What happens then when a person dies?

We know that the body ceases to function. The brain becomes inert and the physical man is dead.

But what happens to the real you — the human personality? What happens to all this information — the memories, thought patterns, and personality traits? When a book is burned, its contents are no longer available. When a computer is smashed, the information within it is also destroyed. Does the same thing happen when a man dies? Is the mind and personality irretrievably lost?

We know that God is omniscient. He knows all and does not forget. God knows every thought and memory that exists within our brains. There is no bit of information that escapes His knowledge.

What, then, happens when a man dies? God does not forget, and therefore all of this information continues to exist, at least in God's memory.

We may think of something existing only in memory as being static and effectively dead. But God's memory is not a static thing. The sum total of a human personality may indeed exist in God's memory, but it can still maintain its self-identity and volition, and remain in an active state.

This sum total of the human personality existing in God's memory is what lives on even after a man dies.

The concept of immortality and of the soul may well be outside the realm of human comprehension. "No eye has seen it other than God." However, our limited understanding of both God and man can provide us with some degree of perception into our ultimate future.

To speak of a concept such as God's memory is indeed very difficult. It involves a deep discussion of the entire transcendental sphere. We therefore give it names that have meaning to us, such as Paradise, the World to Come, the World of Souls, or the bond of eternal life. However, the Bible speaks of immortality as a return to God Himself. "The dust returns to the dust, as it were, but the spirit returns to God Who gave it."

A Deeper Look at the World's Four Stages of Existence

Human history is a progression to a New World Order that will be reached in the Messianic Era. Each individual progresses to his eternal reward in the World to Come via a series of stages that follow earthly death.

←— The Oral Torah teaches that these three eras will take a maximum of 6,000 years.

5774 - We are here

| 1. Olam Hazeh (this world) | 2. Moshiach (Messiah/king) | 3. T'chiyat HaMeitim (Ressurection of the Dead) | 4. Olam Haba (World to Come) |

Olam HaNeshamos (World of Souls)

• The world in which we currently live. • The perfect setting for man to be tested and earn his eternal reward. • The Spiritual World and Hashem's presence are hidden to allow us free choice.	• A flesh and blood descendant of King David unites the Jewish nation, rebuilds the Holy Temple, and becomes king of the Jews. • A 40-year period where the world is at peace. • Man still has material desires and free will, but the knowledge of God is so ubiquitous that evil disappears.	• A literal reuniting here on Earth of individual bodies and souls that were separated at death. • Resurrected people and Creation at large are transformed into spiritually dominant entities that are capable of existing eternally.	• The principal setting for man's ultimate and eternal reward. • A sublime spiritual existence, where man is able to bask in the radiance of Hashem. • An eternal world of truth in which man relives his accomplishments in this world, but from a spiritual perception that is not limited by physical senses.

• Post death, the soul remains in the World of Souls until a "final judgement" that occurs in the Resurrection of the Dead and ushers in the World to Come.
• A place of partial reward, punishment, and purification.** (*Gan Eden* for reward, and *Gehinnom* for punishment and purification)

Note: Gehinnom is likened to a hospital — necessary to remove our spiritual impurities, so we may enter the World to Come and receive our earned reward.

This World and the "Secret of Life"

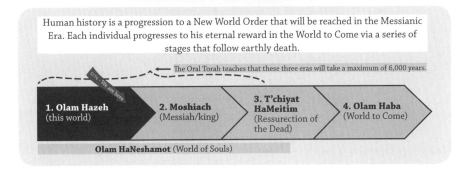

Human history is a progression to a New World Order that will be reached in the Messianic Era. Each individual progresses to his eternal reward in the World to Come via a series of stages that follow earthly death.

← The Oral Torah teaches that these three eras will take a maximum of 6,000 years.

5774 - We are here

1. Olam Hazeh (this world)

2. Moshiach (Messiah/king)

3. T'chiyat HaMeitim (Ressurection of the Dead)

4. Olam Haba (World to Come)

Olam HaNeshamot (World of Souls)

Our present existence is but a preparatory stage for an eternal life of unimaginable sublimeness [sic], the magnitude of which is determined by the individual's conduct in his earthly sojourn.[73]

OUR WORLD INCLUDES SPIRITUAL REALITIES

In His infinite wisdom, God created a world in which His presence is hidden behind the façade we know as nature.[74] This is the ultimate test for man: to see and live with the notion that God is the true Source of all power in the world, or to be drawn into the illusion that the natural world runs by itself.

This is not an easy test because the world was created in such a way

---

73   Appendix to Artscroll's *Talmud Bavli Sanhedrin* (vol. III)
74   *Michtav M'Eliyahu* Book 1

that it seems like man's physical actions are causative. I work hard, therefore I make money. If I don't work hard, I won't make money. Yet, while we certainly need to live in the physical world and play by its rules, it is actually man's spiritual choices that are his true sources of power.

We know that our world contains physical forces and laws of nature. These laws react to physical input and create certain results. For instance, we have all experienced gravity, where something thrown in the air (the physical input) will fall back down to Earth (the result). Physical laws are known from experience and can be measured by science.

Just as we live with these physical realities, so too is our world imbued with spiritual realities. But unlike physical laws, spiritual forces are not readily discernible with our eyes or other physical senses. Still, these forces are very real. Furthermore, these spiritual realities are causative: they determine what occurs in the physical world.[75]

To illustrate, let's consider a computer comprised of hardware and software. The hardware includes the keyboard, mouse, and monitor. When we use the keyboard and mouse, we are providing input into the computer. The software, or rules of operation, then determines what shows up on the monitor.

Our world operates much like a computer. The Physical World is akin to the hardware and the Spiritual World is akin to the software. Each human action, spoken word, or thought effectuates a response in the Physical World. But the way physicality responds depends on the world's spiritual rules. For example, one might work very hard at his occupation and take great care of his body, but his ultimate income and health are instead more influenced by his spiritual inputs (like how he treats other people).[76]

1. We live in a world that is not fully as it appears

During the day, we look up at the sky and are unable to see anything but a bright sky. Is that all there is?

---

75   *Nefesh HaChaim* 1
76   *Ibid.*

No, because at night we realize that an immeasurable number of stars exist.

Many of the forces in our world are not visible to the naked eye. Even though we can't see electricity or magnetism, we can still validate their existence and understand their rules of operation by measuring their impact. If we exert force on a ball by kicking it, it will go in the opposite direction of the kick. While we can't see the underlying rule which is encoded into our world (i.e., Newton's First Law of Motion), it nonetheless exists.

Thanks to advancements in technology, science keeps uncovering rules within our physical world. It wasn't too long ago that humanity was unaware that all matter was composed of microscopic building blocks called atoms. We now know that even a solid rock contains a dynamic world inside where tiny particles are constantly in motion.

Undoubtedly, there are many forces at work in the world that we have yet to uncover and understand. Does the fact that science lacks a complete understanding of our world's operation mean that some of the currently undiscovered forces do not exist?

Certainly not. It's just that we are not sophisticated enough to perceive or measure them.

2. The Spiritual World is causative but connected to the physical

Having been created with both body and soul, we simultaneously live in a world that is both physical and spiritual.

However, since our senses only perceive the physical, it is all too easy for us to go through life without recognizing the Spiritual World. Furthermore, it is certainly not obvious that the Spiritual World actually "powers" the Physical World.

But it does. Not only do spiritual forces exist, they are the true power behind our Physical World. It is the Physical World that responds to our spiritual input!

For example, when we flick a switch and the light goes on, the switch actually has no inherent power. In reality, the switch is connected behind the wall to wires that run out of the house, down the street and ultimately to the power plant, which is the true source of power. If the switch is not connected to the flow of power, the light will not work.

Similarly, a person's physical actions are not the true causative factor for actual results, but rather just the switch at the end of the process. It is the Spiritual World and God that is the actual "power plant." When our actions are not connected to the Spiritual World, blessing does not flow forth. But when our actions are connected to the Spiritual World, our positive influence impacts the entire world.[77]

3. Human beings activate spiritual forces

Thanks to modern science (and specifically Newton's Third Law of Motion), the world recognizes that every action causes an equal and opposite reaction. Although this is a law of the Physical World, it is fascinating to note that it helps explain the Spiritual World as well. God created His world so that each action, spoken word, thought, and emotion has a corresponding reaction in the Spiritual World. The Spiritual World responds to man's input and causes corresponding changes in the Physical World. Even such things as weather, health, and circumstance are influenced by our actions.

On a basic level, the illustration below depicts the interaction of the Physical and Spiritual Worlds:

① An individual goes about his day in the Physical World, experiencing moment after moment.

② Each action, word, thought, and emotion sends data to the Spiritual World.[78]

③ The Spiritual World responds to each action and causes changes in the Physical World. (Note: identifying the exact spiritual re-

---

77   *Ibid.* 1:14
78   *Nefesh HaChaim* 1

sponse to one particular action is almost impossible).[79]

④ Each action leaves an imprint on the Spiritual World (i.e. is recorded).[80] In the World to Come, each person will be able to experience all of his moments simultaneously (and with new powers of spiritual perception.[81])

The Spiritual World responds to input from the Physical World, and then dynamically reconfigures the circumstances of the Physical World.

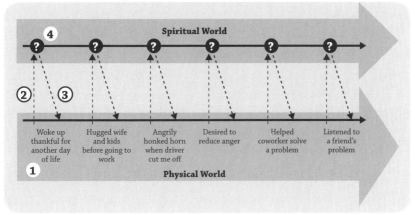

To illustrate how one's actions might dynamically reconfigure the Physical World, let's look at one situation with two different sets of input. *(Note: this is purely for the purpose of illustrating how spirituality can impact the Physical World. This is not to say that God operates the world precisely like this for each person. Circumstances are uniquely tailored for each individual to guide them towards spiritual growth. What inspires one person may not be appropriate for another.)*

Bob is about to drive home from work and the weather has been alternating between rain and snow.

In the first scenario, Bob has been fulfilling his spiritual potential to the best of his abilities and is trying to get home to spend time with

79   *Ibid.*
80   *Ibid.*
81   Introduction to *Ruach Chaim* 4:2

his family. It's possible that the Spiritual World responds by allowing the weather to warm up a degree or two so that Bob encounters light rain, making his commute easy.

Under a second scenario, Bob has not been fulfilling his spiritual potential and wants to get home for negative and/or selfish purposes. It's possible that the Spiritual World responds by having the weather cool down a few degrees. The result is icy roads and many others leaving work at the same time. As a result, his commute becomes long and frustrating.

In both scenarios, Bob influenced his circumstances. Also in both scenarios, the Physical World was affected in the exact way that Bob needed it to be affected in order to help him actualize his potential.

Although the time with his family may have been more enjoyable and rewarding, based on his decision and needs the opportunity to deal with his frustrating commute (and his character trait of anger) offered him great opportunity for spiritual growth.

While we may not be able to measure the impact of any one act or the exact spiritual response, Judaism teaches that the Spiritual World responds to and dynamically reconfigures the circumstances and input of the Physical World.[82] With no doubt, the spiritual response is related to God's will (i.e., Torah and *mitzvos*, as described below).

In other words, positive actions (based on goodness, caring, and spiritual growth) will elicit a favorable spiritual response, while negative actions that contradict God's will elicit a different kind of spiritual response.[83]

This does not mean, of course, that doing the right thing necessarily leads to an easy life — we see this isn't always true. Life is more complicated than that, as we will see below. It *does* mean that positive actions bring blessings and positive results, while negative actions do not.

---

82   *Nefesh HaChaim*
83   *Ibid.* 1

4. Torah and Mitzvos: Rules of the Spiritual World and keys to eternity

We have the ability to measure our Physical World and understand its physical rules. That is why we have science. We do not have the same ability regarding the Spiritual World and its rules. God therefore provided us instructions: the Torah. (In fact the word Torah actually means "instructions."[84])

Mitzvos are the specific actions commanded within the Torah. They teach us how to "operate" the Spiritual World so that maximum blessing flows forth into our lives. Just as an e-mail sent without the proper address will not reach its destination, so too actions that are not aligned with spiritual realities will not trigger the most positive spiritual responses.

Still, the impact of *mitzvos* is much deeper than just triggering spiritual responses.

The term *mitzvah* has become synonymous with both "command- ment" and "good deed." Both explanations are true, but neither provides a full understanding of the Hebrew word's essence.

- We are certainly *commanded* to keep the *mitzvos*, so to translate as "commandment" is accurate. Still, a commandment implies a benefit to the commander with an element of coercion being applied to the commanded. This is misleading because God only commanded us out of love and the desire to give to us. God has no needs. Performing *mitzvos* is fully in our best interest so that we may derive maximum pleasure from this world and the Next World.[85]
- When we perform *mitzvos*, we are indeed performing *good deeds*, so the word is accurate. The problem with the term *good deed* is that people use the word *good* to mean just about anything they agree with. In the Torah's eyes, it is not a subjective standard. While overlap might exist between an individual's definition of

---

84   *Nesivos Olam* (Maharal), Nesiv HaTorah 1
85   Mishna, end of *Tractate Makkos*

good and the Torah's (e.g., helping an old lady across the street), a subjective interpretation leaves the possibility for a person to be influenced by his desires and thus rationalize any behavior as good. Furthermore, without an objective definition of good, how is someone supposed to know how to act when faced with complicated situations (e.g., choosing which life to save and similar situations)?

Another explanation of the word relates to its root. The word *mitzvah* comes from the root *tsavsah*, meaning "to connect with," as in a relationship. In His infinite wisdom and altruism, God set up a world with the potential for us to build a relationship with Him. To the extent man connects with God in this world, so too will he enjoy that relationship eternally.[86]

Mitzvos are the channels God has provided Jews to connect with Him. They are the mechanisms by which Jews can fuse the Spiritual and Physical Worlds. The goal of performing a *mitzvah* is not just the actual *mitzvah*, but the personal growth and enhanced relationship achieved as a result. Since the pleasure of the World to Come is based on the relationship one has built with the Provider of all pleasures, *mitzvos* are, in essence, our keys to eternity.[87]

In other words, each of us creates our own World to Come. How? With each moment of life we have the opportunity to

> **Filling the Hole in Our Soul**
>
> We all have the unconscious desire to connect to our Creator. Without guidance on how to focus that desire appropriately, we inevitably fall prey to a myriad means of fulfillment, which are ultimately unsatisfying.
>
> Many of us feel that there is a huge hole in our soul that needs to be filled. Without doing so, we just don't feel whole. We try all sorts of strategies to fill the void — food, drink, business, entertainment, etc. While these activities can serve a limited purpose, in the long term they don't solve the problem. At its depth, what we are really looking for is God — and the way to access Him is through the Torah.

---

86   *Da'as Tevunos* 126

87   *Derech Chaim* (Maharal), commenting on "The Holy One wished to bestow merit upon Israel...", end of *Makkos*

connect with, or not connect with, God. Each action, spoken word and thought either brings us closer or distances us from Him. Although we cannot perceive it, there is an indescribable spiritual component to each action we take. With every moment, we are "etching data" into the ultimate database, i.e. God's memory. This information, and the associated spiritual benefit, is kept in escrow for us to access after we leave this world.[88]

5. We earn reward by connecting to God

As we saw, God created man in order to share His goodness with him. Our ultimate purpose, then, is to receive that goodness. We do so by connecting to the Infinite. In other words, our primary objective in this world is to form a relationship with God.[89]

By way of analogy, when we first meet a new person it can be difficult to enjoy the time spent together with him. An investment of ourselves is necessary for us to fully appreciate what that person is all about. The more we get to know the person and share common interests, our comfort level and trust increases. As a result, we derive more pleasure from the relationship.

The same is true regarding our relationship with God. The more we invest in the effort to have a relationship, the more we will receive from that relationship. If we make no attempt to know God here, how will we possibly enjoy the fruits of that relationship — either in this world or in the World to Come?

How do we relate to the Infinite? The Torah is the tool that teaches us how to connect with God. We can listen to Him (i.e., learn His Torah) and His messages (i.e., our life circumstances). We can talk to Him (i.e., prayer). Also, we can emulate His ways.

---

88   *Ruach Chaim*, commentary on Introduction to *Avos*: "All of Israel has a portion..."
89   *Mesilas Yesharim* 1

6. Each person has the potential to partner in completing Creation

As described above, each of us has the ability to affect the entire world through our actions. This is an unbelievable concept. Why did God create a system in which man plays such a significant role? Because God wants man to be a partner in the final state of Creation, the World to Come.[90]

Allowing us to help complete the world adds to the pleasure and sense of accomplishment each person will ultimately feel. God places man in a setting that less than complete and provides him the mechanism (i.e., Torah and *mitzvos*) to complete it.

The World of Souls: A Temporary Post-death Abode

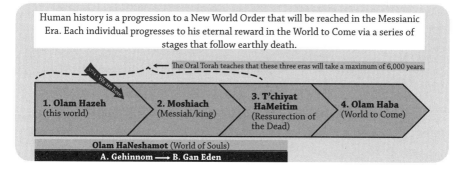

Human history is a progression to a New World Order that will be reached in the Messianic Era. Each individual progresses to his eternal reward in the World to Come via a series of stages that follow earthly death.

⟵ The Oral Torah teaches that these three eras will take a maximum of 6,000 years.

5784 · We are here

1. Olam Hazeh (this world)

2. Moshiach (Messiah/king)

3. T'chiyat HaMeitim (Ressurection of the Dead)

4. Olam Haba (World to Come)

Olam HaNeshamot (World of Souls)
A. Gehinnom ⟶ B. Gan Eden

When a person dies, his disembodied soul enters the World of Souls: the souls of the righteous delight in Gan Eden, whereas [nonrighteous souls first have the opportunity to become purified] in Gehinnom....[In Gan Eden,] the soul attains exalted levels of perception, and rises to greater spiritual heights and attachment to the Divine.[91]

THE WORLD OF SOULS

At death, the soul separates from the body and enters a dimension called the World of Souls. The World of Souls is:

---

91   Appendix to Artscroll's *Talmud Bavli Sanhedrin* (vol. III)

- A temporary existence in which the disembodied soul resides from the time of physical death until the soul is rejoined with the body at resurrection.
- A place of purification and partial reward (We experience full reward during the World to Come).
- Souls that require purification first enter a part of the World of Souls called *Gehinnom*. Depending on the need for purification, souls remain there from one second to one year.[92] Note: souls that do not require purification enter *Gan Eden* directly.
- The soul then enters another part of the World of Souls called *Gan Eden*.[93]

THE SEPARATION OF BODY AND SOUL AT DEATH

Whether the separation of the soul from its body is a painful experience or not depends on how that individual lived his life. One who has led a hedonistic life was too attached to the physical. For this person, the separation of the soul from the body will be as difficult as pulling tangled hair through a comb. On the other hand, for a person who has pursued spirituality and developed sensitivity of the soul, the separation is as easy as pulling a hair out of milk.[94]

Following death, the soul remains close to the body. The soul is disoriented in its new surroundings and the body is very familiar. After a few days, the soul realizes that it no longer has the opportunity to perform *mitzvos* and grow further. It then comprehends that it is destined for greater things and no longer needs the body.[95]

EACH PERSON IS JUDGED THREE TIMES

Shortly after death, each soul is judged according to its deeds in order to determine its reward and punishment in the World of Souls.

---

92   *Eduyos* 2:10
93   See *Even Sheleyma* (Gr"a) 10:12
94   *Berachos* 8a
95   *Zohar* 1:217

Does it need to go through the purification of *Gehinnom*, and if so, for how long? What will its level of reward be in *Gan Eden*?

The other two times of judgment occur every Rosh HaShanah (to determine the person's allotment in this world during the upcoming year) and the Final Judgment (at the end of the Era of Resurrection to determine who will merit what level of eternal life and reward in the World to Come).[96]

THE ENTRANCE EXAM TO THE WORLD OF SOULS

The Talmud[97] indicates that we will be asked a series of questions — an entrance exam of sorts — when we come before the Heavenly tribunal. These questions focus on how we performed against our key objective in life: whether our spiritual essence blossomed or whether we were slaves to our base physical desires. These questions include:

1. Were we honest in business?
   » Were we greedy in our relationships?
2. Did we fix times for learning Torah?
   » Did we spend time learning the real lessons of life (God's objective values in the Torah) and apply them to our life?
3. Were we involved with being fruitful and multiplying?
   » Did we live just for ourselves, indulging our needs and wants, or did we understand our mission here to be for the sake of making a difference for others?
4. Were we anxiously anticipating the redemption from exile?
   » Did we see through the façade of nature and apparently random life circumstances and realize that God controls all (except our free will choices) and that our lives here are a test?
5. Were we intellectually employed in pursuit of wisdom and understanding?

---

96 Sha'ar haGemul (Ramban), *Drashah* on Rosh HaShanah
97 *Shabbos* 31a.

> » Were we striving to perfect our perception of reality or not?

6. Did we have "Fear of Heaven"?

> » Were we living with a daily awareness that we are a piece of Creation absolutely dependent upon a Creator?

(Adapted from Torah.org)

Elsewhere, the Talmud indicates that one of the first questions we'll be asked when getting to heaven is: "Did you taste all of God's fruits?" [98]

While He could have made a more limited world and provided our nutrition in limited ways, God instead made a world of immense variety. He provided us the ability to derive many (kosher!) pleasures from taste and other senses.

The question goes well beyond just whether we enjoyed different fruits or food. More broadly, did we recognize and appreciate all of God's gifts in this world? Did we enjoy the pleasures, blessings, and beauty of God's world?

GEHINNOM — PREPARING THE SOUL TO RECEIVE ITS REWARD

As discussed above, if a person merits eternal life but his soul requires purification, the soul will first enter a part of the World of Souls called *Gehinnom*.[99] Like any corrective process, *Gehinnom* is not a pleasant experience. Although it does partially serve to punish, its primary purpose is purification.

Gehinnom is analogous to a hospital. We don't desire being in a hospital; but if part of our body needs repair, we are thankful such a place exists in order that we can get better and go on living. Similarly, if we didn't live our lives in a way that allowed our souls to partake in the pleasure of the World to Come, thank God there is such a place as *Gehinnom*. Thus, the pain and difficulty is only for the purpose of

---

98   *Mesilas Yesharim* 11
99   See *Rosh HaShanah* 17a

removing barriers to one's pure essence caused by his acts of separation from God. Still, one cannot live life haphazardly here and rely on *Gehinnom* to "do the job" because it will only purify a person in accordance with the level that he has attained in this world.

The amount of purification needed will vary from person to person. To the extent that one's actions removed his ability to connect with God, he will need to be purified.

For example, if a child plays in the sand, his father may simply need to wipe off the sand. If the child played in the mud, however, he may require a more involved cleansing with warm water and a washcloth. And if the child fell into wet cement or a cesspool, he might need to undergo a somewhat extensive cleansing process with abrasive scrubbing and combing.[100]

If a soul does require time in *Gehinnom*, it will spend between one second and one year there. It should be noted that it is possible to be so evil as to not even merit *Gehinnom*. However, this is a rare case. Everyone who makes it into *Gehinnom* has at least some share in the World to Come after his purification. In this light, *Gehinnom* is essentially an aspect of reward.

Non-Jewish representations of hell, which depict a fiery world, likely have their roots in Jewish thought. This is because *Gehinnom* is often described as a fiery existence. However, in Jewish thought, these fires are of a spiritual nature. Kabbalistic teachings include the idea that after death a person will be shown everything he accomplished in this world versus all that he could have accomplished if he had used his time wisely. Part of the spiritual fire of *Gehinnom* is the soul's sense of shame and embarrassment as it realizes what it could have accomplished.[101]

As long as each of us is alive, we have the opportunity to purify ourselves in this world and lessen or avoid the need for Divine (and unpleasant) purification after death. Judaism includes the concept of

---

100 *Toras Ha'Adam*, Sha'ar haGemul (Ramban) 121
101 *Ikkrim* 4:33; *Nishmas Chaim* 1:13

teshuvah whereby a person can repent and change. In addition to lessening (or even removing) the need for purification in the next world, one who strives to improve his ways brings great merit to himself in this world and the World to Come.[102]

GAN EDEN — A MICROCOSM OF THE ULTIMATE REWARD

Once a soul has been purified in *Gehinnom* (if it needed to be), it enters *Gan Eden* and awaits resurrection and the Final Judgment, which determines each individual's eternal reward in the World to Come.

Gan Eden is a place of bliss in which the soul receives incredible reward. Still, the magnitude of this reward is just a fraction of what awaits the soul in the World to Come. The nature of this pleasure is both spiritual and intellectual — the result of a close attachment to God. This pleasure is incomparably greater, and qualitatively different, than the limited pleasures we experience in this world.[103]

Gan Eden also serves to further prepare the soul to receive the ultimate reward in the World to Come.

By contrast, *Gehinnom* serves to remove any blemishes the soul received in this world. But the soul is not yet ready to receive reward to its fullest capacity.

The mystical teachings of Judaism explain that in *Gan Eden*, the soul learns Torah with God.[104] This might be compared to a young child who goes through many years of schooling to prepare for the responsibilities of being an adult. The child goes from level to level, learning new things that enable him to take advantage of life upon completing his schooling. Similarly, the soul ascends from level to level in *Gan Eden* to prepare itself for receiving reward in the World to Come.

---

102   *Yoma* 88a
103   *Toras Ha'Adam*, Sha'ar haGemul (Ramban)
104   *Zohar Chadash*, Rus

DO THE DEAD KNOW WHAT IS HAPPENING IN THIS WORLD?

When someone dies, do they retain awareness of what is happening with the living? Or at death are we in an entirely new realm of consciousness, essentially divorced from This world?

Rabbi Aryeh Kaplan elucidates this idea in his article "What the Dead Think of Us." He writes:[105]

[The Talmud] asks: Do the dead know what is happening in the world of the living?

After an involved discussion, the Talmud concludes that they do have this awareness. The Kabalistic philosophers explain that the soul achieves a degree of unity with God, the Source of all knowledge, and therefore also partakes of His omniscience.

When a man dies, he enters a new world of awareness. He exists as a disembodied soul and yet is aware of what is happening in the physical world. Gradually, he learns to focus on any physical event he wishes. At first this is a frightening experience. You know that you are dead. You can see your body lying there, with your friends and relatives standing around crying over you. We are taught that immediately after death, the soul is in a great state of confusion.

What is the main source of its attention? What draws its focus more than anything else?

We are taught that it is the body. Most people identify themselves with their bodies, as we have discussed earlier. It is difficult for a soul to break this thought habit, and therefore, for the first few days, the soul is literally obsessed with its previous body.

This is especially true before the body is buried. The soul wonders what will happen to the body. It finds it to be both fascinating and frightening to watch its own body's funeral arrangements and preparation for burial.

Of course, this is one of the reasons why Judaism teaches us that we must have the utmost respect for human remains. We can imagine how painful it is for a soul to see its recent body cast around like an animal carcass. The Torah therefore forbids this.

---

105   *If You Were God*, Aryeh Kaplan, *p. 33–35*, OU/NCSY Publications, 1983, with permission

This is also related to the question of autopsies. We can imagine how a soul would feel when seeing its body lying on the autopsy table, being dissected and examined.

The disembodied soul spends much of its time learning how to focus. It is now seeing without physical eyes, using some process which we do not even have the vocabulary to describe... One of the few things that the soul has little difficulty focusing on is its own body. It is a familiar pattern and some tie seems to remain. To some extent, it is a refuge from its disorientation.

Of course the body begins to decompose soon after it is buried. The effect of watching this must be both frightening and painful... This varies among individuals. The more one is obsessed with one's body and the material world in general during his lifetime, the more he will be obsessed with it after death. For the man to whom the material was everything, this deterioration of the body is most painful. On the other extreme, the person who was immersed in the spiritual may not care very much about the fate of his body at all. He finds himself very much at home in the spiritual realm and might quickly forget about his body entirely.

In general, adjustment to the Spiritual World depends greatly on one's preparation in this world. Our traditions teach us that the main preparation is through Torah.

Messiah - Step One in Bridging This World to the World to Come

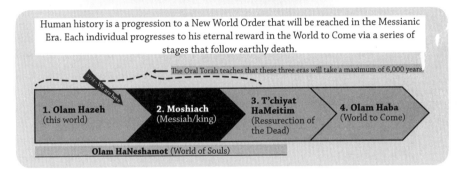

Human history is a progression to a New World Order that will be reached in the Messianic Era. Each individual progresses to his eternal reward in the World to Come via a series of stages that follow earthly death.

← The Oral Torah teaches that these three eras will take a maximum of 6,000 years.

5774 - We are here

1. **Olam Hazeh** (this world)

2. **Moshiach** (Messiah/king)

3. **T'chiyat HaMeitim** (Ressurection of the Dead)

4. **Olam Haba** (World to Come)

Olam HaNeshamot (World of Souls)

Human history is a progression to [a new] world order that will be reached in the Messianic Era... Beginning then, the world will forever be at peace, show obeisance to the Jewish king, seek his counsel...and be filled with the knowledge of God like the waters that cover the sea... Man will still have material desires and free will, but there will be such a general outpouring of the knowledge of God that evil will disappear, and people... will strive to perfect themselves and cleave to God. This idyllic period is the culmination of earthly life [as we know it].[106]

A Jewish king that is the descendant of King David will unite the Jewish nation and lead humanity to the truth of God's Torah. Uniting the Jewish nation involves three primary activities: gathering the majority of

---

106   Appendix to Artscroll's *Talmud Bavli Sanhedrin* (vol. III)

Jews within Israel, rebuilding the Holy Temple, and restoring Torah law in Israel.[107]

Changes will occur in many areas of existence during this epoch which we are told will last forty years. We will list some here:

The World

- This phase is the bridge from the world in which we currently live (which is dominated by the physical) to the Resurrection of the Dead, Final Judgment, and World to Come (which is dominated by the spiritual).[108]
- No miraculous or physical changes occur with respect to the natural world (e.g., the sun and moon remain as we know today).

Man

- Man still has material desires and free will.[109]
- Sustenance will be easy to obtain ("wheat kernels as big as a fist").[110]
- People will use their leisure time to increase wisdom, perfect themselves, and become as close as possible to God.[111]
- Beginning at the onset of this era, there will be no more war and hatred between men.[112]
- The human lifespan will increase. As a direct result of clearly perceiving that God runs the world, stress will decrease and people will live longer.

---

107   *Yad, Melachim* 12
108   *Pesikta Rabasi* 1
109   *Berachos* 34b; see *Shabbos* 63b according to the opinion of Shmuel, while the contradictions in the *Yad, Melachim* ad loc. and ibid., *Hilchos Teshuva*, chapter 8, *halachah* 7. Note: Ramban on *Devarim* 30:6 (see footnote 111) fundamentally argues on the position of Rambam cited here.
110   *Shabbos* 34b
111   Ramban on *Devarim* 30:6
112   *Yeshayahu* 2:4

God

- Humanity will recognize the need to serve God and all people will become willing to collaborate in order to accomplish this end and benefit the world.[113]
- The understanding of God will be so total and fill the world that evil will eventually disappear.[114]

OUR WORLD VERSUS THE DAYS OF MESSIAH

There are two major distinctions between today's world and the Days of Messiah. Although no major physical changes will occur during this era:

1. The Jewish nation will no longer be subjugated to the nations of the world — a state which prevents us from fully appreciating and serving God.

During the Messianic Era, the Jews will no longer suffer prejudice and hatred from the world at large. The removal of this subjugation will facilitate the unity of the Jewish People. And a result, Jews will no longer have this barrier preventing them from achieving their ultimate purpose: to learn Torah, perform *mitzvos*, and become closer to God.[115]

2. Our *yetzer hara* (evil inclination) will be reduced. As a result, we will naturally desire to serve and remain connected to God.

Despite a reduction in our evil inclination, some element of free choice and the ability to choose evil must still exist. In our current world, most people don't have the inclination to murder, but the free choice to do so *does* exist. Similarly, in the Messianic Era, Jews will overcome their negative inclination to ignore Torah and *mitzvos*. Then, we will be imbued with the desire to do God's will. The result of doing God's will is that one purifies his physical self and the world at large.

---

113 *Yeshayahu* 11
114 *Ibid.*
115 "Ma'amar HaGeulah" (Ramchal)

Spirituality will begin to overtake physicality. Although the lessening of the evil inclination will diminish man's free will, he will still receive reward for choosing to learn Torah and perform *mitzvos*.[116]

WHEN WILL THE MESSIAH COME?

According to the Jewish tradition, this world, including the Messianic Era, the Era of Resurrection, and the Final Judgment (i.e., everything up until the World to Come) will last a maximum of 6,000 years.

At the time of this writing, we're in the year 5774. Given that the Messianic Era is a forty-year period, he will come by 5960. We are quite close to the perfection of our world.

Note: We can't know exactly when these events will occur, as they're hidden from us. If we are meritorious, they'll happen sooner.[117]

THE NUMBER FORTY

In Jewish thought, the number forty alludes to the concept of re-creation. The forty-year Messianic Era will recreate our world. During this time, our world will begin to transition from the physically dominant world that we know to a spiritually dominant world that hasn't existed since Adam, Eve, and the Garden of Eden (before the sin).[118]

Throughout history, the number forty has been connected with events involving creation, recreation, and purification. A few examples include:

- 40 days of embryonic development (for a fetus to go from conception to human form)
- 40 weeks of pregnancy

---

116   *Netzach Yisrael* (Maharal) 46
117   *Sanhedrin* 98a
118   Ramban on *Devarim* 30:6

- 40 days of rain in the Great Flood to purify and recreate the world
- 40 years that the Jews were in the desert to purify them from the negative effects of being immersed in Egyptian culture
- 40 days Moses spent on Mount Sinai receiving the Torah
- 40 measures of water in a *mikvah*, the purpose of which is spiritual cleansing and purification

"THE THIRTEEN PRINCIPLES" AND THE MESSIAH

Maimonides (Rambam) — one of the greatest Jewish philosophers and codifiers of Jewish law — compiled Thirteen Principles of Faith. According to Jewish thought, these thirteen principles represent the ideas one must be aware of and accept to properly relate to the Almighty and His Torah. The idea of Messiah is included as one of these thirteen principles. Messiah is necessary as the mechanism (the catalyst) for us to transition from the current world to an eternal world of peace.[119]

As we have seen, true life is the state of being where one is connected to the Source of life (God), while sin is the state of disconnection from the Source of life.

As God is currently hidden, we have a limited ability to connect to Him in this world. Many fail to realize that the Jewish People are currently living in exile. Despite the comfort and the feeling of freedom in many parts of the world, today's world is not the optimal setting for Jews. Without God's overt presence, we lack the ability to experience the world at its highest level and have true peace of mind, world peace, meaning, and the ability to grow spiritually.

---

119   Rambam, Commentary on the Mishna, *Sefer Mitzvos Katan* first *mitzvah*

Resurrection - Step Two in Bridging This World to the World to Come

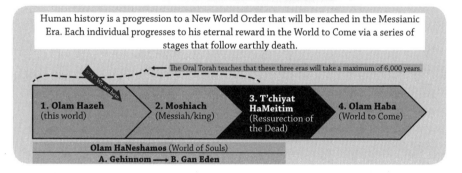

Human history is a progression to a New World Order that will be reached in the Messianic Era. Each individual progresses to his eternal reward in the World to Come via a series of stages that follow earthly death.

The Oral Torah teaches that these three eras will take a maximum of 6,000 years.

5774 - We are here

1. Olam Hazeh (this world)

2. Moshiach (Messiah/king)

3. T'chiyat HaMeitim (Ressurection of the Dead)

4. Olam Haba (World to Come)

Olam HaNeshamos (World of Souls)
A. Gehinnom ⟶ B. Gan Eden

It is a fundamental tenet of Judaism that God will at some point literally resurrect the dead, reuniting here on this earth the body and soul that were separated through death.[120]

Once the world has attained a high level of spirituality and been purified to a great extent (from the Jewish People performing Torah and *mitzvos* in the Messianic Era), God will literally bring the dead back to life.

---

120 Appendix to Artscroll's *Talmud Bavli Sanhedrin* (vol. III)

Some of the characteristics of this Era are:

Man

- At the beginning of this era, people will still live and die as we know today.
- Concurrently, a resurrection process will begin. Souls that have been in the World of Souls will be reunited with their bodies.[121]
- As a result, the world population will become mixed with "normal" and resurrected people. Eventually, the generation of normal people will all die and only the resurrected will exist.[122]
- Man will no longer have free will as we know it today.
- Bodies (though different than our bodies today) will still exist, but physical urges will no longer dominate the individual.
- The fully purified state man reaches at the end of this Resurrection Era is the final, eternal state. It is the resurrected person that enters the World to Come.

The World

- Creation at large is transformed into a spiritually dominant world (wholly unlike our current world) that is capable of existing eternally in the World to Come.
- All moments that have transpired in world history are resurrected so that the maximum holiness (which was not revealed in this world) can then fill the world.

God

- Everything and everyone naturally desires to perform the will of God to the point where physicality no longer has its own independence, but instead is fully subservient to the spiritual.

---

121   *Leshem ad loc.* and onward
122   *Ibid.*

UNDERSTANDING RESURRECTION

To those not familiar with the idea, resurrection (*T'chias HaMeis-im* in Hebrew) may sound like something conjured up from a fantasy novel. The concept has become further distorted, thanks in part to popular movies that depict zombies emerging from graves in a less-than-human state of being.

The Jewish understanding of resurrection is simply the notion of something dying and then being brought back to life by God.

This paradigm of "regrowth" and development into a new form is commonplace within our natural world.[123] We see many illustrations of metamorphosis in our world. For example, we plant seeds into the ground and expect growth. After planting, there is an almost total decomposition of the seed before it begins to grow into a plant. The seed slowly begins to decay, and just as it has reached its greatest point of decomposition, when the seed appears dead, that is precisely when it begins to sprout. Another example is caterpillars who enter their chrysalises and emerge in a different form and with the ability to fly.

Nature is indeed miraculous. If we weren't accustomed to seeing these things happen, they too would sound like fantasy to us. But while science has provided explanations of how many things work, nature also contains various properties that we still don't fully understand. Just as we plant a tiny seed and it can grow into a tall tree, perhaps a similar thing can happen with planting a body in a ground, although it might take a little longer. This is much closer to the Jewish outlook.

DEVELOPING THE SEED OF ETERNITY

According to Jewish teachings, death is a new beginning. It is the birth of the soul. Just as the womb requires a gestation period of nine months before a human is born into this world, this world requires a residence of seventy or eighty years before one's soul can be born into

---

123   *Sanhedrin* 90b

the World of Souls and, eventually, the World to Come.

Before the sin in the Garden of Eden, the human body had the potential for eternal life. After the sin, the body became limited. Death was introduced into the world as the cure for the body to reattain its original form, capable of living eternally and receiving God's full reward.

Death is also a point of conception, and the body can be viewed as a seed. It is planted in the earth at burial for the purpose of a regrowth into a form that can subsist forever.

Our current world, therefore, is about man creating the seed for his eternal life via his free will choices and actions. A healthier and stronger seed results in a more powerful growth for the plant.

The analogy of seeds and resurrection is not accidental. They represent eternity. Seeds, and the trees they produce, possess an aspect of continuity not found elsewhere within nature. Each of a tree's seeds has within it the ability to replant itself and bring forth an entire tree with all its nuances, which in turn contains the ability to replicate ad infinitum.

Furthermore, a tree trunk divides into many branches, which in turn sub-divide further into many smaller branches. Similarly, man has within himself the seed for eternal life and the ability to begin and continue a lineage. We produce children with the innate ability to procreate. This aspect of continuity is why the Torah likens man to a tree.[124] If a little seed can become an awe-inspiring 300-foot tree, how much more so will the regrowth of a human being bring forth!

WHO WILL BE RESURRECTED?

Our tradition teaches that every Jewish soul makes it to the Resurrection of the Dead. However, based on what each soul accomplished in this world, there are different levels of difficulty to get there, as we have seen.

Interestingly, while all Jewish souls make it to the Resurrection

---

124 *Devarim* 20; *Tiferes Yisrael* (Maharal) 7

of the Dead, not all bodies merit resurrection. As alluded to in the section on reincarnation, it is theoretically possible for a person not to have advanced his soul at all. In that case the entire soul will return to a new body and it will only be the new body/soul combination that merits resurrection.

While this book doesn't specifically address non-Jews, Jewish tradition teaches that righteous non-Jews certainly merit a portion in the World to Come.

The resurrection process is about bringing back to life everything about a person (i.e., all of one's experiences) and connecting it with eternal life.

We are familiar with entropy, the concept that all matter is constantly decaying/dying. During the Era of Resurrection, the opposite occurs. It is a purification process where all who have died become infused with life that is fully connected to God's will and eternity.

IN WHAT FORM WILL WE RETURN?

We know that the Next World will be primarily spiritual. Yet, there are various discussions in the Talmud about physical concepts at the time of resurrection. What will a person look like? Will there be eating and drinking? Will a person be young or old? What will I look like if I was deformed? What if I was ugly or beautiful? Will the dead arise with clothes?[125]

How can we approach this difficult concept?

While a person's body does return at resurrection, it is not the same body as today. To exist in the Next World, the body must be of a spiritual nature. It must be fully subordinate to the soul and able to connect with eternal life. Today, the soul is almost imperceptible and the body is clearly visible. The opposite will occur at resurrection. The body will be a barely visible, translucent outer covering that has no connection to evil and allows the soul to radiate through. This bodily

---

125   *Sanhedrin* 90b

covering of the soul is what the Talmud refers to when indicating that people will be resurrected "clothed."

Additionally:

- At resurrection, we will enjoy the company of all the relatives and friends we had in this world.[126]
- People will be resurrected with their distinguishing physical characteristics and blemishes (in order that they are recognizable) and then at some point be fully cured.
- The resurrected will neither desire nor experience lower-level, temporal pleasures such as food or sleep. Instead, people will be sustained by a sublime form of spiritual nourishment.[127]

THE IMPORTANCE OF THE BODY

Resurrection is another of Maimonides's Thirteen Principles of Faith, so we can be sure that the body is of great importance. Why?

We live in a very physical world, but our primary purpose is spiritual: to connect with our Creator. Our bodies were created as the tool for us to connect. Much like scuba gear allows a diver to explore the underwater world, it is the body that allows the soul to exist in the physical world and perform the actions that connect us with God.

Angels (spiritual beings with no connection to physicality as we know it) have no opportunity in this regard. The potential to learn Torah, grow spiritually, and perform *mitzvos* and good deeds is only realized through the body. Consequently, the respect accorded to the body is immense.

BURIAL AND CREMATION

Burial is a critical step in the transition from this world to the Next. Man was created from earth. Once the first man, Adam, sinned and disconnected humanity from the Source of life, man's task in this world became physical.

---

126   *T'chiyas HaMeisim*
127   *Berachos* 17a

As opposed to the spiritual work Adam was originally intended for in the Garden of Eden, today, man must physically toil in this world to achieve his potential. Once he has done so, he can return to the earth and attain his eternal reward.

As we have seen, the body is very important, and burial is a type of planting. For these reasons and more, cremation is diametrically opposed to Jewish belief and law.[128] The Jewish view is that in this world we are merely trustees for our bodies. They are loaned to us as a vehicle to accomplish our objective of spiritual growth and are not ours to do what we please.

Similarly, Jewish law also prohibits self-mutilation, tattoos, and suicide. We are also required to keep our bodies healthy. The body is not to be abused or disrespected.[129]

THE THIRTEEN PRINCIPLES AND RESURRECTION

The idea of resurrection is **not** that the dead will be brought back to life to resume their same lives.

Instead, the concept is that everyone who ever died will be brought back to live lives of spiritual perfection. This means that every single moment of history will also be resurrected to reveal the spiritual potential it contained. The Era of Resurrection is about living again correctly — according to the spiritual truths God implanted into our existence. This era of living correctly will activate the purification necessary to transform our earthly world into a spiritual dimension capable of entering the World to Come and eternal, blissful life.

Why is Resurrection such a critical element of Jewish belief? It teaches us that every single moment of existence is valuable and that with each moment we have the ability to complete Creation.

---

128 *Yad Chovel U'Mazik 5:1, Shulchan Aruch Choshen Mishpat 420:32, Sanhedrin 46b, Shulchan Aruch Yora De'ah 348:2*
129 *Iggeros Moshe*

BODY AND SOUL ARE PARTNERS

Man is not just a soul trapped in a temporal body. If that was so, resurrection would be returning the soul to its "bodily prison."

Rather, man is the fusion of body and soul, and man's goal is to use his soul and intellect to subdue the bodily drives and guide his actions. By themselves, neither the soul nor the body can accomplish much of anything. A body without its soul/life force is inert, while a soul without a body cannot achieve anything in the Physical World.

Interestingly, because neither the body nor the soul can achieve anything independently in this world, each might argue that it cannot be held accountable for its actions. The Talmud provides an analogy of a blind man and a lame man to counter this line of reasoning:

A king of flesh and blood had a beautiful orchard, which contained early figs [i.e. luscious fruits]. And he stationed in [the orchard] two guards, one lame and the other blind. The lame one said to the blind one, "I see beautiful early figs in the orchard. Come, mount me on your shoulders and together we will bring [the figs] here to eat them." The lame one mounted the back of the blind person and they brought [the figs] and they ate them. Some days later, the royal owner of the orchard came and found his prized figs missing. He said to [the guards] accusingly, "The beautiful early figs — where are they?" The lame one said to him, "Do I have any feet with which to travel to the figs? I certainly could not have taken them." And the blind one said to him, "Do I have any eyes with which to see where the figs are? I certainly could not have taken them." What did [the king] do? He mounted the lame one on the back of the blind one, and he judged them as a unit. So too, on the Day of Judgment, the Holy One, Blessed is He, brings the soul and injects it into the body, and judges them as a unit.[130]

Because the body and the soul are partners and act in concert in this world, they must be judged together and receive reward together in the Next World.[131]

Without the concept of resurrection, we might ignore the body

---

130   *Sanhedrin* 91a
131   *Ibid.*

altogether and focus exclusively on the needs of the soul, like the Eastern guru who sits on top of the mountain engaged solely in contemplation, separate from the Physical World.

This is not how the Torah views the purpose of life. Instead, we are supposed to be involved in the Physical World. The physical actions we perform concretize our spiritual ideals and objectives, thus transforming them from potentiality to actuality. This empowers their eternal existence.

WHEN WILL RESURRECTION OCCUR?

Resurrection will begin at some point after the onset of the Days of Messiah. Although the forty-year Messianic period starts first, the Days of Resurrection can overlap with it. Since, as we've seen, the Messianic Era will start in less than 300 years, we are close indeed to this era as well.[132]

---

132   *Leshem ad loc.*

The World to Come - Our Eternal Existence

Human history is a progression to a New World Order that will be reached in the Messianic Era. Each individual progresses to his eternal reward in the World to Come via a series of stages that follow earthly death.

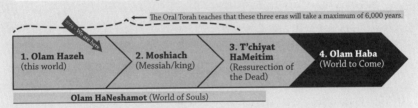

← The Oral Torah teaches that these three eras will take a maximum of 6,000 years.

5774 - We are here

1. Olam Hazeh (this world)

2. Moshiach (Messiah/king)

3. T'chiyat HaMeitim (Ressurection of the Dead)

4. Olam Haba (World to Come)

Olam HaNeshamot (World of Souls)

Our present existence is but a preparatory stage for an eternal life of unimaginable sublimeness, the magnitude of which is determined by the individual's conduct in his earthly sojourn.[133]

The World to Come is the time of receiving reward. It is not a different *place* from our current world, just a different *dimension* that is beyond our concepts of space, time, and physicality.

The Torah tells us very little about what the World to Come will actually be like. In fact, the written Torah only alludes to it, whereas the oral traditions (encapsulated in the Talmud) discuss its existence and some of the fundamental concepts.

Yet, even the Talmud doesn't describe what it will be like. This is not to keep us in suspense; because the pleasures of the World to Come are

---

133 Appendix to Artscroll's *Talmud Bavli Sanhedrin* (vol. III)

infinite, as physical beings we do not have the faculties to appreciate them. However, we do understand that the World to Come is:

- An infinite and eternal world.
- The principal setting for man's ultimate reward.
- A sublime spiritual existence, where man is able to bask in the radiance of God[134].
- An existence of being, where no actions are performed and we simply experience the pleasure we've earned from our accomplishments in this world.
- A world of truth in which man relives his accomplishments in this world, but with a spiritual perception not limited by physical senses.
- An eternal state of Resurrection of the Dead.

AN UPSIDE-DOWN WORLD

The Torah describes the World to Come as an "upside-down world."

The Talmud relates that Rabbi Yosef passed away briefly and then was revived.[135] After his recovery, his father asked him what he saw while he was in the Next World. Rav Yosef answered: "I saw an upside-down world. I saw higher ones below and lower ones above."

Rav Yosef understood that people who were "high up" in this world (who received all the honor and respect) often occupied the lowest positions in the World to Come.

Those who were "low-down," however, who were neither noticed nor highly regarded in this world, were granted what they truly deserved for all to behold.

Rav Yosef's father answered, "My son, you have seen a clear world."

Those who receive the most honor and respect in this world are not necessarily the ones who will be honored and respected in the World to Come.

---

134   *Berachos* 17a
135   *Pesachim* 50a

In fact, the Talmud is teaching us that it is likely to be quite the opposite. The ones who receive the most honor in the World to Come are the ones that have maximized their spiritual potential in this world. These are individuals who weren't concerned with material strivings and personal honor. Instead they were focused on learning and applying Torah, helping others, and personal growth.[136]

WHO MERITS THE WORLD TO COME?

The Talmud states that all Jews have a share "in" the World to Come. As we've seen, righteous non-Jews merit it as well.

While alive, no Jew can become completely disconnected from the Spiritual World and eternity. Even those with a lifetime of negative actions and no connection to spirituality maintain a spark of holiness within themselves. They can still get back on track and acquire and even increase their portion in the World to Come.

As discussed earlier, a person may need to go through a purification process for those elements of his soul that remain damaged upon death. To the extent that they lack good deeds and Torah, the eternal reward will be smaller, but they will still make it to the World to Come.

HOW BIG IS THE REWARD?

Since God is Omniscient (all-knowing) and His judgment is perfect, each person's reward will be precise according to his merits. Still, in terms of what type of pleasure a person will experience, "not an eye has seen."[137] We really can't conceive it. This is because the spiritual reward of the World to Come is not measurable in the currency of this world's physical pleasures. It is not even describable in our world. We can no more fathom the pleasure of the World to Come than the blind can know the beauty of color. It will be qualitatively different than

---

136   See *Shmuel I* 2:3
137   *Yeshayahu* 64:3

anything we currently perceive with our sensory faculties and limited intellect.

Although we can't relate to infinite pleasure and an infinite world, we can at least appreciate our inability to appreciate something much greater by using the analogy of a blind person.

Imagine living in our world without seeing. Then one day you wake up and are able to see. It would literally be a change in the entire scope of what existence means.

Right now, we lack the ability to perceive much deeper levels of this world. After death and resurrection, we will have a new sense (or senses) and, as a result, a heightened ability to perceive what we have produced here, however on the level of eternity.[138]

All pleasure in this world is limited. This includes spiritual pleasures. Even while we're enjoying something it is tempered by the fact that it will or could end at any time.[139] But in the World to Come, we will experience infinite and eternal consciousness. The pleasure will not be limited by the possibility of it ending. At the same time, the World to Come will not be a static existence. Instead, the World to Come will be characterized by a continually increasing measure of pleasure — a journey from one level of pleasure to the next.

Because the spiritual reward of the World to Come is qualitatively different than physical pleasures, one moment of pleasure in the World to Come can be greater than all the pleasures of this world combined.[140] In other words, if it were possible to combine all the pleasure experienced by each person who ever lived, it would still pale in comparison to one moment of eternal pleasure.

WHAT ARE ETERNITY AND INFINITY?

We currently live in a world of time and space. As the Torah teaches, time and space are actually creations of God that He lives outside

---

138   *Pirkei Avos* 4:17; Sha'ar haGemul (Ramban)
139   *Avodah Zarah* 65
140   *Avos* 4:17

of. As physical beings in our current world, we are limited by time and space and cannot conceive what infinity is like. As a result, we experience events sequentially and longitudinally. While we may remember past events, and may even be significantly impacted by some of them, for the most part they come and go and get incorporated into our overall essence.

To describe the timing of events in our lives, we use the terms *past, present*, and *future*. In reality, there is no such thing as the "present" because once you contemplate it, it's gone. These "present" moments continuously disappear with the passage of time. And because these moments quickly become part of the past, they are essentially dying in the physical world.

However, they live on in the eternal world of intellect, and so our real opportunity in this world is time. We have the ability to "export" each moment of our lives to the World to Come, much like the way someone toiling in a gold mine has the ability to collect riches for later use.

When the average person thinks of infinity, he probably thinks of a never-ending series of moments that come and go. This is not real infinity since each of these moments is finite. Even if we were to live forever, that would not be true infinity.

If we think of a train with a thousand cars, someone standing on the platform would see each car of the train one by one as it passes by. This is similar to how humans experience time one moment at a time. But if someone were on top of a mountain, he could see all of the thousand cars of the train at once, because he is above the train. Similarly, God is outside of time and has awareness of all moments in our 6,000-year world within His "present" knowledge. In other words, unlike the human experience of sequential moments, God sees all events at once.

In the World to Come, we will also exist outside of time. As a result, we will be able to experience all events at once, as well as experience the cumulative impact of each of our actions.

What is the difference between living one moment at a time (as we do in this world) and having access to all moments at once (as we will in the World to Come)?

Our experience of moment-to-moment time is limited. If we cover a map with a piece of paper containing a hole in the middle, we see only one city at a time. But we know that the whole world is behind the piece of paper. Similarly, all of our past moments are hidden from us, but nonetheless have left an imprint on our being and cumulatively influence us. Just as removing the sheet of paper allows the viewer to see the whole map at once, so too, when we leave this world, we will see our whole life with all its moments coexisting, with light and dark corresponding to the choices we made.[141]

WHO WILL YOU SPEND ETERNITY WITH?

Everyone we have ever associated with will be part of our eternal existence. Because God is Omniscient, not a single moment gets lost. The more we've interacted with someone in this world and the stronger the bond we've created (e.g., family and friends), the stronger the relationship there will be in the Next World.

THE FINAL JUDGMENT THAT USHERS IN THE WORLD TO COME

Every person is judged three times (although, at a certain level, everyone is judged constantly). These times are:

1. Every Rosh HaShanah regarding his life and fortune in this world.
2. At death to determine his need for purification and reward in the World of Souls.
3. The Final/Great Day of Judgment that occurs at the end of the Era of Resurrection and ushers in the World to Come and determines our eternal level of reward.[142]

---

141   *Michtav M'Eliyahu*
142   Sha'ar haGemul (Ramban), *Drashah* on Rosh HaShanah

Whenever a person is judged, he is judged based on his individual situation. What was his situation? What were his challenges? What tools he was given to accomplish his personal mission, and how did he respond given all this? No two people have the same mission or the same set of circumstances. All factors are precisely accounted for.[143]

Each of us is put in precise life circumstances and is given the exact tools and abilities to successfully accomplish our custom-made tasks in life. Those who have fulfilled their potential will be amply rewarded while those who fall short will be held accountable. We are not judged objectively as to whether we have quantitatively accomplished as much as another person. Instead, we will be measured against how well we fulfilled our potential.[144]

So, can we really say that a rabbi has earned more reward than a thief?

Since the ultimate reward in the World to Come is determined based on how significantly an individual fulfilled *his* or *her* potential in this world, it's possible that a thief who was raised in a family of murderers has overcome great obstacles to become an ordinary thief who tries not to hurt anyone. He might very well have achieved more in this world than a rabbi who has not grown to his full potential.[145]

Why is a final judgment at the end of time necessary when a person has already been judged at his death? After all, there has been no free will since death, so what is there to get rewarded for or purified from?

A final judgment is necessary because the ultimate impact of one's actions cannot be measured until the end of time. After death, one's actions still impact others and add to (or God forbid subtract from) what he merited. A prime example of this is with parents and children. Parents significantly influence their child's actions. Often, this holds true long after a parent dies. To the extent that a child performs worthy deeds after the parent dies as the result of the parent's influence, the parent will continue to accrue merits even after death.

---

143   See *Shmuel I* 2:3
144   *K'sav V'HaKabbalah, Parshas Balak,* on the verse "Not one man..."
145   *Even Shelayma* 1

Why Is The Afterlife Relevant?

What if you knew that after your death you would spend the next 500 years on the North Pole?

Would you not spend some time while still alive visiting your future existence, scoping out the living conditions, building a house, gathering resources, and making other preparations in order to make it more habitable?

This analogy is akin to the purpose of our life in this world: to make spiritual preparations for an eternal existence. The question we need to ask ourselves on a regular basis is: what spiritual luggage are we packing ourselves for eternity?

In short, the World to Come is relevant because:

1. Life in this world is finite,
2. An eternal Afterlife awaits us, and
3. Our decisions and actions in this world determine our eternal existence.

1. Life in this world is finite

We live in a world in which we are unable to change two known truths: we are born against our will and we die against our will.

As a result, each individual's life is essentially a riddle. And most people, at least at some point during life, consider this riddle by asking themselves several questions: What am I doing in this world? And what happens after I leave this world?

These can be scary questions because most of us have a fear of death, at least on a subliminal level. For the most part, we are more afraid of the prospect of nonexistence than we are of any temporary pain we may experience upon death itself. This is so because our lives, until that point, are the only existence we can know with absolute certainty.

Think about it: Do you remember being in your mother's womb? None of us do.

In the same way that leaving the womb and being born into this world is not really "dying," leaving this world is also not really "dying." What people call "death" is really the process of being born into a better world. Rabbi Tucazinsky describes this in more detail and provides the analogy of two brothers in the womb in his work *Gesher Hachaim* — the Bridge of Life:[146]

Life on this earth begins with man being transported from the womb of his mother and ends with his restoration to the earth from which he was formed and to which he must return. This life on earth constitutes no more than a bridge between two basic forms of life — the past and the future... We call this bridge through which we pass "life," the emergence from the womb "birth," and the return to earth "death." The reason for this nomenclature is that man is only aware of the substance of his present life. He is incapable of forming any conception of a spiritual life, one unassociated with physical functions. He no longer knows anything of his past and having no idea of the long future ahead, man views this short transition period as his entire world, with nothing behind or beyond.

During those early months when man is hunched over with his head between his legs within his mother's womb, his mouth closed, and his food all prepared and ingested through his navel (and, according to the sages of the Talmud, enjoying a sublime and enlightened life), were he to be mentally developed to the same degree as human beings outside the womb

---

146   p. 27–30, Moznaim Publishing Corp, 1983, with permission.

are, he would regard his mother's womb as the only world... He could not imagine a world extending beyond the expanse of the womb.

Now suppose there were twin brothers lying together in the womb who could think and ask each other what would happen to them once they left their mother's womb. They would not be able to form any conceptions whatsoever of what awaited them — of all their eyes would see and their ears hear here on earth.

Let us imagine that one of them believed in the tradition he had received that there was a future life beyond the womb, while the other, a "rational" being, would only accept what his own intelligence could grasp, and he, accordingly, would only acknowledge the existence of what he experienced of " this world" [in the womb] alone. The two would disagree and argue, very much as men do on earth — some believing that man continues to live, others denying that man has any life other than in this world of the present.

Suppose the "believing" brother were to repeat what had been transmitted to him: that with their emergence from the womb they would enter a new and more spacious realm; that they would eat through their mouths, see distant objects with their eyes, and hear with their ears; that their legs would straighten; that they would stand erect and traverse vast distances on a gigantic nurturing earth, replete with oceans, rivers, and more, while above them would stretch a sky with its starry hosts.

The other, who only believed in what he could sense, would jeer at his brother's naiveté in indulging in such fantasies. He would retort that only a fool would believe all of this nonsense, which makes no sense to the rational mind. The more the "believer" elaborated on the variegated features they would encounter after leaving the womb, the more the "rational" brother would mock and ridicule him.

The believing brother would ask, "What then, my enlightened brother, do you believe is in store for us when we leave the womb?"

"It's simple and obvious. Once this enclosure opens and you are torn away from this world where your food and drink are provided, you will fall into an abyss from which there is no return. You might as well never have existed at all," the "rational" brother would reply.

In the heat of their argument, the womb suddenly opens. The "naïve" brother slips and falls outside. Remaining within, the other brother is shattered by the "tragedy" that has overtaken his brother.

"Brother, where are you?" he calls. "How did you manage to fall to your destruction? Your folly that these contractions were birth pangs caused your downfall. That is why you did not clutch at anything to stop yourself." As he moans the misfortune, his ears catch the cry of his brother, and he trembles. To him this spells the end, the last gasp of his expiring brother. Outside, at that very moment, joy and celebration fill the home of the newly born baby. "Mazel tov, Mazel tov, a baby... We have a son!"

Just as the life of the embryo merely constitutes the transition to a broader and more exciting life, so, to an even greater extent, is life on earth merely the prelude to a more fascinating, glorious life which man, confined within his puny body and with limited perception, is incapable of conceiving.

However great the difference between life in the womb and our present life may be, the difference which the soul will ultimately find between this life and that of the world to come is immeasurably greater...

The "enlightened" brother could never believe that his brother had not died, that he had, instead emerged from a miniscule to a vast world. Even were he endowed with the intelligence of the wisest of men, he could never grasp what would happen to him after he would fall from the womb.... Similarly no human being can ever grasp the nature of the life led by the spirit once it becomes detached from the body. The person who believes that his flesh and bone are the very substance of life and that life ceases once they disintegrate and revert to their previous state is similar to the "rational" embryo, philosophizing in his mother's womb...

Life in the womb is like being in the antechamber of a palace hall below of finite dimensions, while life on earth is a corridor to the infinite palace above.

The term "death" has a negative connotation largely because science cannot measure and prove the existence of the Afterlife. Yes, death is very sad for the living who have just lost a loved one.

Still, death is not a final event, but rather *a temporary separation of body and soul*. Just as leaving the womb is the process to enter a better world filled with enhanced consciousness and pleasure, so too is leaving this world.

Making this mental shift from seeing death as the end of life to seeing it as the beginning of eternal life can have a profound impact on a person. If we were certain that another more brilliant existence were to follow this one, how much more comfortable would we be in this world? The more a person understands why he was put in this world, what the purpose of death is, and what the World to Come is all about, the less he will fear death. And when a person does not fear death, his whole perspective on life changes; he can truly experience life without the ultimate anxiety. Peace of mind and a calmer attitude will permeate his essence.

Furthermore, when we realize that death is just the beginning, being aware of our mortality can actually be quite empowering. This recognition has the ability to put one's entire life into proper perspective. This sentiment is frequently communicated by those who have had near death experiences and have thereby received "second chances" at life — their lives become richer. Across the board, these people develop a deep sense of gratitude and enhanced meaning. They appreciate being alive more than they used to. They are better able to cope with and face their challenges in life.

Because it is not the end of our existence, death is misconceived as being finality. In reality, it is the beginning.

In one aspect, though, it does indeed represent finality. The Oral Torah (in Ethics of our Fathers) describes this world as the time of accomplishing and the Next World as the time for receiving reward. In this world, a person is granted free will to improve himself, to improve the world he lives in, and to improve his connection to the Source of life (i.e., God). Once he leaves this world, he will neither have free choice nor the ability to improve himself. He forever loses the ability to make free will decisions, to perform more good deeds, and to alter his eternal state of being. He will exist eternally on whatever level of spirituality he has set into motion.

2. An eternal Afterlife awaits us

"One moment of bliss in the World to Come is better than all the life of this world" (Ethics of our Fathers, Chapter 4, Mishna 22).

How can we have confidence that a transcendent existence — one that is more "real" than this one — indeed awaits us after death?

Have you ever had a dream that was so vivid, so real, that you experienced it as if it were reality, but then you woke up, possibly in a cold sweat or with a burst of energy?

Events like this remind us that this world is not the ultimate reality. After death, we will awake to an even "more real" reality, and our experience in this world will be like a dream to us. This is one reason that the Talmud describes sleep as one-sixtieth of death: so that we can taste the World to Come in this world. In his book *World Mask*, Rabbi Akiva Tatz describes[147] how everything in this world serves to teach us something about the Spiritual World. Included in this elucidation is the perplexing question of dreams. If this world is really just an illusion and the Next World is the ultimate reality, why is there a need to contain an illusion (i.e., a dream) within that illusion?

All of this world is analogy for a higher reality. Each detail of the world teaches something about its source in the Spiritual World; each detail is an exact parallel of that which exists there. This is perfectly logical: if we were commanded to study and understand the spiritual realm and yet had no avenue of access to that understanding, what would be the sense of such a command?...

Just as a person observes the physical body of his friend in order to relate to the person or the inner being of that friend, so too we study the structure and movements of the physical world in order to perceive its root... Just as we can perceive the human soul by means of its vehicle, the body, so too can we begin to perceive the Divine root of the world by the

---

147   p. 66–68, Targum Press Inc, 1995

means of that vehicle, that body which we call the world... Consider images projected on a screen: the forms and figures moving on the screen are no more than light dancing in two dimensions. They may look very convincing...but in fact those images are very distant visions of the people and places photographed to produce them. However... they are exact replicas of the original. They may be entirely illusory compared to their sources, but one who carefully studies that light dancing on that screen will recognize those people and places when he meets them in the future... Similarly, one who studies this world well is studying that which is a distant representation of a source which cannot be seen from here. But one day in the future, on that inevitable day when the transition must be made from this world to another, the one who has studied well will recognize every detail of that reality. Then it will become apparent that this world, for all its beauty and sense of reality, is an analogy for the Divine Source of that reality...

So we understand that all of our experiences are projects of reality which teach us about that reality. If this is true, then we must face a perplexing question: if every human experience is an illusion relative to its source in the higher world, what is a dream? What does a dream teach us about reality? If our experiences here are relatively illusory, why would Hashem have created us with dreams as part of our lives? A dream is all illusion; why put illusion into the illusion? Let us understand: in a dream, one is not aware that one is dreaming — the dream seems very real, sometimes ecstatically pleasurable, sometimes terrifyingly traumatic. The very intensity of these feelings is due to the fact that one perceives them as fully alive and real. And yet when one wakes, perhaps sitting up in bed in a sweat generated by the torment of a nightmare, one is relieved to realize that what one has just gone through was only a dream. Why do we need this experience of the unreal which seems so real?

The answer is clear and illuminating. Imagine for a moment an uninformed person being told about the nature of life in this world and the transition from this world to the next. Imagine that such a person is being told: "You should know that this world is only an illusion relative to the next. It may seem real, but do not be fooled — one day, sooner or later, *you will leave this dimension and enter an entirely different one. There you will realize that all you have experienced in life was a very faint echo of the reality you perceive there. That is real life; whatever you knew before was almost nothing in comparison to it."*

The person being told this story would probably reply: "That sounds wild! How can I accept such an idea? Surely it is more reasonable for me to see the world in terms of what meets the eye right now; how can I believe that all my awareness of the world is only an illusion? That is simple outside of my experience and outside of all the evidence available to me. I reject such fanciful and unsubstantiated stories!"

And one would certainly be excused for replying thus! A person could not possibly be expected to doubt his perception of the world with which he has such solid contact. Since all his senses assure him that his experience of the world is true and reliable, he could not think otherwise.

Unless he has ever had a dream! Anyone who has ever dreamed has experienced the remarkable transition from what seems completely real to a state in which it is obvious that the reality of which he was so sure a few seconds before was entirely an illusion! After living through a few vivid dreams a person must be faced with a very unsettling thought: when you dream...you awake and realize that it was only a dream and that you are now awake. But are you sure? How can you be sure? How do you know that you are awake now? Because you simply know, you can feel clearly that you are awake? But in your dream you were certain that you were awake too!

Anyone who has dreamed has experienced the priceless gift of feeling in the flesh, in the most immediate way: that the state of being which we call life in this world has no inherent assurance of being objectively real and permanent... A dream is a humbling experience. And it is the key to belief in a world after this one; it is an experience in this world that should sensitize us to the idea that there is more to life here than meets the eye. No one who has dreamed can possibly deny that with any confidence at all. And so even a dream, that experience of illusion, teaches about reality!

3. Our choices determine our eternal existence

This world is comparable to the antechamber before the World to Come. Prepare yourself in the antechamber, so that you may enter the banquet hall.

(Ethics of our Fathers)

A story is told of a poor man, who in need of supporting his family, travels to a foreign land. On the way, his ship sinks in the stormy sea, and he luckily makes it to a nearby island. Much to his amazement, he sees that the island is literally covered with diamonds. There are diamonds on the beach, diamonds on the side of the road, diamonds everywhere.

In an effort to return home, he finds a shipbuilder and offers to pay him in diamonds to build a boat. The shipbuilder laughs and says, "What am I going to do with worthless diamonds?" The stranger thereafter learns that the currency of value on the island is meat fat. Working very hard over a number of years, he earns enough meat fat not only to pay for the building of a boat, but also to have plenty to bring back with him. When his boat is finished, the traveler loads it up with meat fat and heads home.

When he arrives home, his family is overjoyed to see him. Proudly, he announces, "We are now rich!" He opens the hatch of the boat and shows them all the meat fat he accumulated! A loud silence fills the air as the poor man realizes his tragic mistake.

(Adapted from Aish.com)

To a certain degree, each of us is similar to the person in this story. A person is brought into this world to grow spiritually. But, given the pace of life and the abundance of on-demand entertainment in today's world, we get distracted from our real task in life. Too often, whether it be choosing career over family or the immediacy of physical pleasures over deeper pursuits, a person finds himself trading diamonds for meat fat. Unfortunately, it is only after leaving this world that most of us will fully appreciate this.

The Jewish belief is that each individual creates his own World to Come with his actions in this world. It's an amazing thing and hard to envision, but God has created a system whereby at each moment a person has the power to create his own eternity.

In this world, a person lives inside space and time and thus experiences events sequentially. We see each moment come and go. What we do not see is how each thought, word, and action leaves its fingerprint on the Spiritual World and is "recorded" by God. In the World to Come, a person will come face to face with all of his moments. He will experience the impact of all these moments together, but from a spiritual perspective. The person who has lived his entire life focused on physical ends — and not optimizing the precious resource of time — will not have accrued many spiritual moments with which to enjoy his eternal existence.

DEVELOPING OURSELVES FOR THE WORLD TO COME

In the womb, a fetus develops eyes, ears, a nose, and a mouth, despite the fact that it cannot see, hear, smell, or taste. These physical organs and senses develop solely for use in the post-birth existence that follows the womb.

The same thing happens in this world. Each person develops spiritual faculties that he won't be able to fully access or utilize until he dies. But in contrast with the baby in the womb, growing these new faculties is an active opportunity, a choice that each of us must constantly make.

Can you imagine living in our world without fully developed eyes or ears? They are amazing tools we are blessed with so we can appreciate and perceive the world more clearly.

Who has a deeper appreciation and perception for the game of golf: the first-time hacker or the one who has invested the time to learn the components of a golf swing and fine-tune his short game? So too do wine connoisseurs, classical music lovers, and chess aficionados gain more pleasure from their respective pursuits than their lay counterparts.

And the same is true for the Next World. If one does not develop his spiritual faculties and the ability to connect with the Creator sufficiently in this world, how much will he truly appreciate the World to Come?

FINAL THOUGHTS

The Jewish concept of the Afterlife is a state of being, not doing. In the World to Come, we will experience everything we've accomplished in this world, but on a spiritual plane without physical limitations. There is nothing new created there.

Each individual enjoys what he has created with his efforts in this world. And this is precisely why the current world is so important. We have a limited time to exercise our free will — and then we live off the spiritual fruit we've planted forever.[148]

Continuous spiritual growth is not easy. But according to Jewish thought, this is the purpose of the Jewish nation: "to be holy and a light unto the nations…to perfect the world."[149] The challenge exists for all of us to continuously improve ourselves and the world we live in; to transcend morality and aspire towards holiness.

Every physical action counts. Science has shown that the flap of a butterfly's wings in Australia might result in a storm in North America. What we do has an impact.

How much goodness might come into the world as a result of our next act of kindness?

The cover of this book conveys the main takeaway of belief in an afterlife, which is that life is but a path. The path is not always smooth.

While journeying on the path, we may not be able to clearly see where it leads.

But there is one thing in our control: to decide whether we're heading towards a setting or a rising sun.

---

148 Sha'ar haGemul (Ramban), *Drashah* on Rosh HaShanah
149 Aleinu Prayer

Bulk copies of this book are available at significant discounts for educational purposes.

About Mosaica Press

Mosaica Press is an independent publisher of Jewish books. Our authors include some of the most profound, interesting, and entertaining thinkers and writers in the Jewish community today. There is a great demand for high-quality Jewish works dealing with issues of the day — and Mosaica Press is helping fill that need. Our books are available around the world. Please visit us at www.mosaicapress. com or contact us at info@mosaicapress.com. We will be glad to hear from you.

MOSAICA PRESS

ח. חמשה מיני ערב רב יש בישראל. א' בעלי מחלוקת ולשון הרע. ב' בעלי
תאוה. ג' הצבועים שאין תוכם כברם. ד' הרודפים אחר הכבוד לעשות
להם שם. ה' הרודפים אחר הממון. ובעלי מחלוקת הם גרועים מכולם
והם נקראים עמלקים. ואין בן דוד בא עד שימחו מן העולם. וכל מחלוקת
שלא לשם שמים. הוא מערב רב הקופצים להורות ולטול עטרה. כמו
שכתוב ונעשה לנו שם כו'.

ט. בכל דור ודור שולט מדה אחרת (ממדותיו של הקב"ה שמנהיג
בהם עולמו) שמזה משתנים הטבעים וכל מעשי הדור והנהגותיהם
ופרנסיהם הכל הוא לפי ענין המדה ההיא ותלוי בבחירתם בין טוב
לרע וכן הנהגות הקב"ה עמהם, והכל כלול בתורה, (וז"ש שהראה
הקב"ה לאדם הראשון וכן לאברהם דור דור ודורשיו, רוצה לומר
שהבין הכל מהתורה.) וכן בכל דור ודור יש קצים לפי ענין התשובה
והזכויות המיוחדים לאותו דור. אבל קץ האחרון לא תלוי בשתובה
אלא בחסד, כמו שכתוב למעני למעני אעשה. וגם בזכות אבות. וזהו
שאומרים וזוכר חסדי אבות ומביא גואל לבני בניהם למען שמו.
וזה הקץ לבד נתגלה לאבות. וזהו שאמרו ללבי גליתי. רוצה לאמר
לאבות ולמשה שנקראו לבי.

י. כל העניינים שבחודש תשרי הם רמז לעתיד לבא. כי מתחילה הוא
יום הדין בראש השנה. ואחר כך סליחת העוונות ביום הכפורים.
ואחר כך סוכות. ושמיני עצרת ושמחתן [נ"א שמחת תורה]. וכן
לעתיד לבא תחילה יום הדין הגדול ואחר כך וזרקתי עליכם מים
טהורים וטהרתם כו', כי אסלח לאשר אשאיר. ואח"כ בסוכות חופות
שבע כידוע. וכמו שכתוב וסוכה תהיה לצל יומם כו'. זמן שמחתינו
כו' ועמדו זרים ורעו צאנכם ואחר כך שמיני עצרת תהיה לכם ויאכלו
שלש סעודות של שבת. היינו סעודת בהמות בהררי אלף. וסעודת
לויתן. ויין המשומר כו'.

יא. סעודת לויתן. הוא הדעת שתתרבה בארץ שהוא השמחה הגדולה אשר
אין למעלה ממנה. וכן משה רבינו נקרא לויתן ועל זה נאמר יצרת לשחק
בו והוא השעשוע של הקב"ה עם הצדיקים שמחדש להם התורה כו' וכמו
שכתוב ויחזו את האלקים ויאכל וישתו. והראיה הוא ההשגה. והוא האור
הגנוז לצדיקים ויהיה פנימיות התורה בהתגלות כמו עכשיו פשוטו של
תורה. ועל כן יהיה חירות מכל המקטריגים, וכמו שכתוב לא ירעו ולא
ישחיתו כו' כי מלאה הארץ דעה כו' וכן יין המשומר הוא סודות התורה
שיתגלו על ידי משה. ועל אותו הזמן נאמר יהי כבוד ה' לעולם ישמח ה'
במעשיו במהרה בימינו כן יהי רצון.

פי"א בעניני ערב רב וחבלי משיח, ועניני גאולה העתידה במהרה בימינו

א. ארבעה עניני גאולה יהיה בארבעה פרקים שהעולם נידון. היינו בפסח יגאלו מהשעבוד. ובראש השנה תהיה גמר הדין באויבי ה'. ובעצרת יהיה קבוץ גליות על ידי משה רבינו ע"ה. ובסוכות בנין בית המקדש.

ב. מתחילה יגאלו עשרת השבטים, ואחר כך שבט יהודה. ואחר כך יחיו דור המדבר.

ג. הגאולה הזאת לא תהיה רק על ידי למוד התורה. ועיקר הגאולה תליא בלימוד הקבלה.

ד. בזכות שמתרחקים מאותן העוסקים בלמוד פילוסופיא אלקית, לימודיות. וטבעיות. יזכו לעתיד לבא לאור ה'.

ה. הגאולה מכונה בשם בוקר, כמו שכתוב אתא בוקר וגם לילה, וכן מכונה בשם לידה כמו שכתוב כי חלה גם ילדה ציון כו', וכמו שקודם שמתחיל להאיר היום הוא מחשיך ביותר. וכן ההרה כשמתקרבת הלידה כואבת יותר מכל ימי הריונה כשיושבת על המשבר. כן קודם הגאולה יכבד הגלות יותר מכל הגלות.

ו. כמו שבתבואה יש שלשה מיני פסולת מוץ ותבן וסובין. כן בישראל שנמשלו לתבואה כמו שכתוב ראשית תבואתו. נמצאו שלשה מיני פסולת שהם ישמעאל עשו וערב רב. ונגד אברהם ויצחק שמהם יצאו עשו וישמעאל יבואו שני משיחים שהם משיח בן יוסף ומשיח בן דוד. והם יברכו את ישראל ממוץ ותבן כו'. ויהיו כמוץ לפני הרוחק ובית עשו לקש. אבל עדיין לא יהיה בירור גמור עד שיבררו מן הערב רב שהם נגד הסובין שהם דברים בחטה מאד. והם הפסולת שכנגד יעקב (והם נגד ביטול תורה ופריקת עול מלכות שמים). והם דבוקים מאוד בישראל וישראל לומדים ממעשיהם. והם העשירים עליזי גאותך (ועליהם אמרו אין בן דוד בא עד שיכלו גסי הרוח מישראל כו') וכמו שאי אפשר להפריד הסובין מהקמח עד שתטחון התבואה היטב, כן אי אשפר להפריד הערב רב רק על ידי קושי הגלות.

ז. לפי שהדורות מתמעטין והולכין והערב רב מתגברין. לפיכך הוצרכו חכמי הדורות בכל דור ודור לגזור גזירות וסייגים חדשים לגדור הפרצה שפרצו הערב רב.

וגם כוכבים ומזלות ומלאכי השרת כולם מצטערים ובוכים עם הנשמה
לפי שהיא ניטלה מכולן ובמעשיה פגמה בכולם ועשתה בהם חושך וכולם
לוקין עמה. ושם בגיהנם מתודה ומצדיק הדין ומתפלל להעלותו משם
בזכות הצדקה שעשה קודם מותו ואחר שיסבול הכל מוליכין אותו לגן
עדן ומשם שולחין אותו בגלגול לתקן עיוותותו.

לג. עיקר גן עדן הוא מים. ועיקר גיהנם הוא אש. ובב׳ יסודות אלו משתמשים
העליונים. והתחתונים משתמשין ברוח ועפר. והאדם צריך לעבור בכולן.

כב. בעין רשום כל העולם וכל אשר בו. וכל מה שעושה טוב או רע נרשם באותו מקום שבעין בצורתו ודיוקנו ואותו יום וזה שמראין לאדם לפני מותו.

כג. הסטרא אחרא תרדוף לשלם לאדם תיכף כרעתו אבל הטוב צפון לצדיק עד שנשלם.

כד. אף על פי שלאחר גזר דין אין התשובה מועיל להצילו מן המיתה מכל מקום מועיל להעלותו מגיהנם אחר שיסבול הכל.

כה. מי שמת קודם י"ג שנה. הוא על פי משפט ב"ד של מעלה (על עוונות אבותיו). ומכ' שנה ואילך הוא על עוונות של עצמו. אבל מי שמת מי"ג עד כ' שאז אינו בר עונשים ש"מ ע"ז נאמר יש נספה בלא במשפט אבל מ"מ הכל בצדק.

כו. אע"פ שאמרו שאין ב"ד של מעלה מענישין עד כ' שנה, מ"מ אחר כך נענש על הכל. (וז"ש שמח בחור וכו' ודע כי על כל אלה יביאך אלקים במשפט)

כז. גן עדן הוא בדרומית מערבית של העולם. וגיהנם בצפון.

כח. הצדיקים מצפים על החכם בעוה"ב שיגיד להם חידושי תורה וכשבא הצדיק לגן עדן נותנין לו ק"נ ימים לדרוש ברבים התורה שלמד בעוה"ז.

כט. לעתיד לבא יטהר הגיהנם מטומאתו ויוכלל בגן עדן. ושניהם יוקבעו בארץ ישראל.

ל. כמו שלמטה בבית המקדש יש מדריגות מדריגות. מקודם נכנסין להר הבית. ואחר כך לחיל ולעזרת נשים. כן הוא למעלה. וכמו שכתוב ה' מי יגור באהלך כו'. והאדם במעשיו בעוה"ז בונה שם כמה מזבחות שבכל עולם. שעליה מקריבין נשמתו.

לא. הקב"ה ברא את האדם להטיבו באחריתו. ואף אם האדם חטא הקב"ה מחזירו לזה העולם פעמים ושלש עד שיתקן מה שעיות. ונותן אותו בגיהנם עד שיזדכך ויעבור ממנו הזוהמא. אך החילוק הוא כי מי שהיה טוב מתחילה גופו זוכה ג"כ לעוה"ב. אבל מי שלא תיקן מתחילה. הגופים הראשונים כלים ונאבדים ומי שאינו מתקן בפעם הד' אז אבדה תקותו רח"ל.

לב. מתחילה מוסרין את הרשע למלאך דומה שהוא ממונה על המתים בקבר. ואחר ג' ימים מוסרו דומה לגיהנם שהוא בעמקי הארץ לצרפו ולזככו. ושם משעבדים בו החיצונים. וכ"א נוטל חלקו ממנו עד שיעלה גביתם וכל צער שהנשמה מצטערת בגיהנם גם הגוף מצטער ובוכה עמה בקבר.

לפניו וי לפלוני דמריד במלכא וגידון אז. הג' כשמכניסין אותו לקבר נידון למעלה. הד' הוא חיבוט הקבר נידון כל אבר ואבר שנהנה בעוה"ז שלא במצוה. הה' דינא דתולעתא ונפשו עליו תאבל. הו' כף הקלע בעבור דברים בטלים. ונעשה רוח (וגם עבור החמדה). הז' הגיהנם.

יב. ג' דינין עוברים על האדם עד שיבא לגן עדן. והוא יום הדין וגיהנים ואימת מות כמ"ש דנפישי ביעתותא דמלאך המות ואח"כ יבא לגן עדן.

יג. האדם הנוסע ממקום למקום יש בזה ג' מקומות. היינו המקום שהוא נוסע ממנו. והמקום שהוא נוסע לשם שהוא תכליתו. ומקום דרך הנסיעה. וכן הוא באדם. העוה"ז שנסע ממנו. ומקום תכליתו הוא הגן עדן. ודרך הליכתו. שא"א לבא לגן עדן אף אחר שיקנה שלימות עד שיתפשט מן הגופניות.

יד. בג' דרכים צריך לליך אחר המיתה. במדבר. בישוב. בים.

טו. י"א מסעות צריך האדם לנסוע עד שיבא למקום מנוחתו, דהיינו א) מביתו לקברו. והב) הוא מקבר לגיהנם. שאף אם הוא צדיק גמור צריך לעבור בגיהנם. והג) מגיהנם לגן עדן. ומג"ע לז' רקיעים. ומשם לג"ע העליון. ובכל מקום צריך ליתן דין וחשבון.

טז. נהר דינור מפסיק בין ארץ ישראל של מעלה לחו"ל כמו הירדן למטה והוא גיהנם של מעלה. וקודם שנבנסין לג"ע העליון צריך לעבור בנהר דינור.

יז. ד' מיני הגעלה יש. דהיינו ליבון באור. והגעלה בחמין שהוא מים ואש. וטבילה בצונן. וכלי חרס שבירתן מטהרתן. וכנגדן ד' מינים. היינו צדיקים. בינונים. ורשעים. במים שהם רשעים גמורים. וכשעוברים בנהר דינור כל א' נידון שם לפי מעשיו דהיינו צדיקים נידונים שם בצונן. ורשעים באש. ובינונים במים ואש דהיינו חמין. והולכים אחר נפש הבהמיית הולכין לאיבוד. כי כלי חרס כיון שנשברה אין לה תקנה.

יח. על ידי הרחיצה בנהר דינור מסירים מעליו הבגדים צואים שהוא לבוש עוה"ז. ששם נכלו האברים והגוף. ואחר כך מלבישים אותו במלבושים שתיקן לו מהמצוות. ועולה לקרבן על ידי מיכאל שהוא כהן של מעלה. וזוכה לעמוד שם תמיד לפני ה' וליהנות מזיו השכינה.

יט. אף על פי שהקב"ה מעניש נכנס לפנים משורת הדין. אבל הרע לבריות משלמין לו כגמולו ממש וכן להגבה לב.

כ. הרע לבריות אינו עולה מן הגיהנם עד שיעלוהו הצדיק. והרע לשמים אינו יכול ליכנס לגן עדן עד שיבא הצדיק.

כא. האברים מעידין על האדם והימים הם בגדים צואים שבהם נידון וכן לטובה שמקבל בהם שכר.

פ"י בענין שכר ועונש וגן עדן וגיבהם והדינים אשר יעברו על האדם עד בואו למקום מנוחתו.

א. כל עושר עוה"ז הוא מטרפי אילני דג"ע ואין צדיק אוכל פירות בעוה"ז אא"כ יש צדיקים הרבה בדור, ודוקא אם הוא טוב לבריות.

ב. הפירות של הצדיק אין נותנין לו רק לבניו.

ג. צדקה ומפשט הם דלתות התורה. ושכר הצדקה עושר. ושכר משפט אמת הוא ממשלה. ומי שאינו עושה משפט וצדקה מפסיד אף העושר וממשלה שמגיע לו ממצוה אחרת.

ד. כבוד הוא עוה"ז הגרוע ועושר שעושה בעשרו מע"ט הוא יותר טוב מעוה"ב. ופעמים שהקב"ה נותן ממון לאדם כדי לפדות עצמו מן היסורים.

ה. לצדיקים מצפינים גם שכר הפירות לעוה"ב לטובתם.

ו. שכר המצות הוא בלתי תכלית. וגמול עונות הוא בתכלית.

ז. הס"א מתחילה נראית לו כאוהב והפתי הולך אחריו כל ימיו וכאשר היא יורדת ליטול נשמתו אז הוא סובר שבאת עכשיו ג"כ למלא תאותו אבל היא הופכת לו עורף וממיתה אותו.

ח. הרשעים אפילו בשעת מיתתן מקשים ערפם ולוחמים עם המלאך המות אבל הצדיקים פושטין צוארם כיונה (ומתכוונים לקיים בזה רצון הבורא יתברך).

ט. כל הימים מדת הדין מקטרג ואין שומעין לה עד יום המיתה.

י. בעת המיתה אז הוא יום הדין החזק מאד כמ"ש (צפניה א') יום ה' הגדול וכו' מר צורח שם גבור. והנשמה (קודם מותו היא ברגלים וצריכה לעלות לגרון) בבית הבליעה. ואז מוכרח לראות השכינה בין צדיק בין רשע רק ברשע השכינה מסתלקת תיכף ואז מצער אותו המלאך המות מאד ויוצאה נשמתו כפיטורי כפי וושט, אבל בצדיק אין שכינה מסתלקת ממנו עד שמוליכתו למקומו ונשמתו יוצאה בנשיקה וג' אבות יוצאים לקראתו (והם נגד ג' מלאכים הבקרים מעשיו וכמ"ש לקמן סי' י"א)

יא. ז' דינין עוברין על האדם והם א' תיכף קודם מיתתו באים ג' מלאכים. א' חושב כל הרגעים שהיה בעולם ונוטל חשבונו מה עשה בהם. והב' חושב העבירות שעשה והג' שלמד אתו תורה בבטן אמו ועכשיו בא לראות אם הם שלימים אותו. הב' הוא אחר המיתה כשמוליכין אותו לקבר מכריזים

ספר
אבן שלמה

נוסד לפלס דרכי התורה והעבודה במאזני צדק, ולפנות
מהם כל אבני מכשול, וגם עוד איזה ענינים נפלאים.

מיוסד על מקראי קדש ומאמרי חז"ל כפי שביארם
לאמתה של תורה הרב הדומה למלאך ה' צבאות הגאון
החסיד האמתי רבן של כל בני הגולה איש אלקים קדוש
המפורסם בכל קצוי ארץ מורנו **אליהו מווילנא** זצוק"ל
מלוקט עם הערות על ידי הרב הגדול המפורסם מורנו
הרב **שמואל** ב"ר **אברהם מאלצאן** זצ"ל

פֶּרֶק י' – י"א